**DEDICATED TO
MY DAD, MOM, AND FAMILY**

Contents

ACKNOWLEDGEMENTS

Writing a book is always a very intense and time-consuming process. I have been in the computer networking field for more than two decades. Preparing for technical interviews is always cumbersome. It requires reading multiple books or watching numerous videos on various training websites. What we do in the real world helps but technical interviews always have some textbook questions. No matter how good you are at your work, you will still be judged based on some bookish concepts. So, this book is an effort to summarize most major technologies and concepts in one place.

I would like to thank my parents Prof. D.P. Sharma and Anu Sharma for being my teachers and inspiration. I also want to thank my mentor G.K. Agarwal. I used to call him GK uncle. In 1995 he gave me the opportunity to work in Computers departments for Ford now Farmtrac. It was GK uncle's motivation that laid the foundation for my career.
I am also grateful to my colleagues and friends, including Santhosh Sridhar, Faisal Shah and Francis Luong, for providing valuable insights and feedback on this book. Several sections of this book, including the MPLS and BGP sections, are the result of our technical discussions.

I am grateful to both Krish Sharma and Daizy Bali for their exceptional work, their commitment to excellence, and their unwavering support throughout this journey. Without their expertise and guidance, this book would not have been possible. I also want to thank Sonia Sharma for re-reading this book several times to provide feedback. Thanks to Rajbir Kaur and Himanshi Nagpal for cover design. A big thanks to my daughter Jasmine for sacrificing some of her time that we use for our joyous musical drives.

I would like to extend my heartfelt thanks to all the readers for your support and interest in this book. It is your enthusiasm and encouragement that keep me motivated to write, and I am honored to have the opportunity to share my work with you. Thank you for being a part of my journey as an author, and I hope that this book will help you in your networking career.

1 Networking Basics

In this chapter, I will focus on networking basics. I know, I mentioned in the title that this book is a deep dive. However, when we study advanced technologies, we sometimes forget some very basic concepts. For example, as a network engineer, you know that you spend most of your time on layer three of the OSI model. Of course, you know that layer three is the network layer, but do you know all seven layers of the OSI model? If you do, that's awesome; if you don't, I have you covered. In this chapter, I will cover several terminologies which network engineers use in their day-to-day support and troubleshooting.

Networking is based on a seven-layer OSI model. OSI stands for Open Systems Interconnection. An OSI model has seven layers. Please understand that this is all conceptual. We use this model to divide the responsibilities of technical professionals and it defines boundaries for different technologies. It also ensures the interoperability of various network devices operating on various OSI layers. I am starting from the seventh layer - Application, Presentation, Session, Transport, Network, Data Link, and Physical layer.

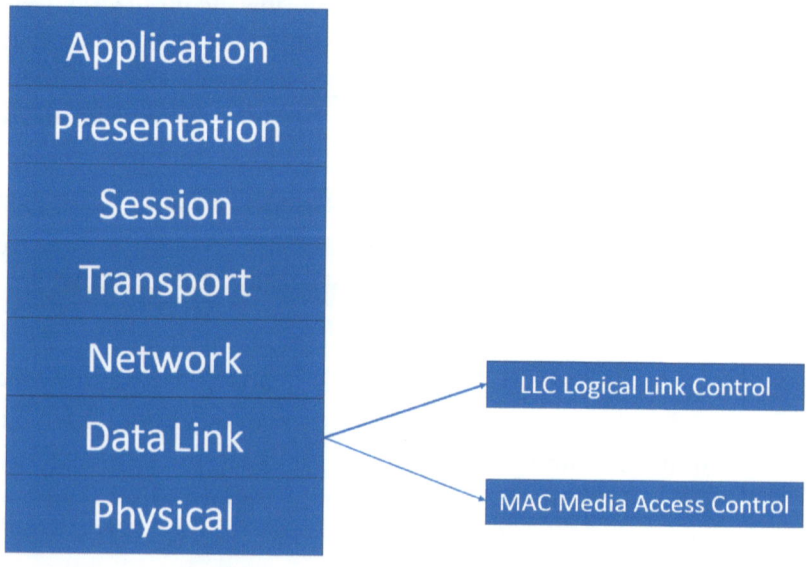

Network engineers spend most of their time working with Layer 1 (Physical), Layer 2 (Data Link), and Layer 3 (Network). Network security engineers work on layer 4 (transport) as well.

Physical Layer

The physical layer is the first layer of the OSI model. This includes network hardware such as a router's port, line cards of modular routers, cat 5 or 6 cables, fiber cables, NIC for computers, etc. This list is endless. However, I will discuss some very commonly used network hardware components in modern data centers.
Most networking environments use three different mediums for transmitting data traffic. These three mediums are Copper, Fiber, and Air. At this point, wireless is out of the scope of this book. I may add it in later editions.

Copper

Copper cables are also called Cat 5 / Cat 6 cables and can handle distances up to 100 meters, and bandwidth of 1000Mbps or 1Gbps. Copper can support 10Gbps for an approximate cable length of 55 meters.

Fiber

Now let's discuss some common fiber optics standards used in data centers.

Multi-mode

Multimode fiber is also called short reach. The range or length of cable depends on the bandwidth and the type of cable being used. A multimode can support distances ranging from 100 meters to 550 meters.

Single mode

Single mode fiber, also known as long reach, can handle up to 100 Gbps and it supports distances from 5km to 120km.

Data Link Layer

The second layer in the OSI model is the data link layer. Switches are layer two devices. Switches use MAC addresses to facilitate communication on a network segment.

Anatomy of MAC Address

A MAC address is also known as a physical address. A device on the network has two types of identifications, MAC address/Physical address and IP address / Network address. MAC address has 48 bits.
The first 24 bits of MAC signify OUI. OUI stands for the organizationally unique identifier. Network device manufacturers buy OUI from the IEEE (Institute of Electrical and Electronics Engineers).
The second set of 24 bits is assigned to a networking device by the manufacturer.

IP Addresses

An IP address is also called a network address. This resides at layer 3 of the OSI model. An IP address is comprised of 4 octets. Each octet has 8 bits. So, an IP address has 32 bits in total.

Subnet Mask

Let's understand the subnet mask before we discuss the details of IP addresses. A subnet mask signifies the number of bits assigned to the network.

A subnet mask is a 32-bit number that has network bits set to 1's and host bits set to 0's.
Class A subnet mask 255.0.0.0
Class B subnet mask 255.255.0.0
Class C subnet mask 255.255.0.0

Let's take an example of Class A, here first 8 bits are set to 1.

11111111.00000000.00000000.00000000
  255   **0**   **0**   **0**

If you convert the above octets into decimal numbers, it will be 255.0.0.0.

There is another way, we can express subnet masks. For example, if a subnet mask is /12, it means out of 32 bits, the first 12 bits are set to 1s, and they are representing the network. The remaining 20 bits are set to 0s, and they are representing hosts. This representation is also called classless IP addressing scheme. (/12 is called slash 12) I know, you may be laughing at "slash 12". Not many new network engineers know that.

IP Addresses

An IP address is a unique identifier assigned to every device connected to the internet. It is a 32-bit binary number that is usually represented in decimal format, known as dotted decimal notation. IP addresses can be categorized as follows:
Class A – 1.0.0.1 to 126.255.255.254
Class B – 128.1.0.1 to 191.255.255.254
Class C – 192.0.1.1 to 223.255.255.254
Class D – 224.0.0.0 to 239.255.255.255
Class E – 240.0.0.0 to 254.255.255.254

Private IP Addresses

There are IP addresses that can be used on private networks without registering with the internet registrar Arin. These IP addresses are called private IP addresses. Private IP addresses are defined by the RFC1918 standard. These IP addresses are not reachable through the internet.

Here are private IP address ranges:

Class A 10.0.0.0 to 10.255.255.255
Class B 172.16.0.0 to 172.31.255.255
Class C 192.168.0.0 to 192.168.255.255

Classful IP Addresses

Classful subnets are traditional subnets, such as class a, class b, or class c. This means we can have /8, /16, and /24 subnet masks. Now
imagine a scenario where we have two routers connected back-to-back. We need only two IP addresses for this network. If we use a classful network, the best choice will be /24 and we will use two IP addresses and the rest of the IP addresses will be wasted. That's where classless IP addressing scheme comes in handy and it helps in conserving the IP addresses.

Classless IP Addresses

Classless subnetting is the answer to the above-mentioned problem. It is also known as CIDR, Classless Interdomain Routing. We can divide /24 into smaller chunks. We can get a /30 out of /24. That way we will use only two IP addresses. The rest of the IP block can be saved for future IP assignments.

IPv6 Addresses

I think this book will be incomplete without talking about IPv6 IP addresses. You may wonder if 4.3 billion IPv4 addresses were not enough for the internet. A quick google search took me to wired.com website, that states "There are about 10 billion devices in the world, connected to the internet." IPv6 is 128-bit IP addressing scheme that offers 340 undecillions (340 Trillion Trillion Trillion) unique IPv6 addresses.

Prior to deep diving into IPv6, I will give you some IPv4 comparisons. This will help you in memorizing this new way of IP addressing. If you remember, for point-to-point connections, in IPv4 we have /30 or /31 subnet mask. Like /30 in IPv4, we have /126 in IPv6 that provides four IPv6 addresses. IPv6 uses /127 subnet that provides two usable IPv6 addresses for point-to-point links just like /31 in IPv4.

Now I will pick a random IPv6 address, and I will simplify it for you. Let's have a closer look at the following IPv6 address:

2001:0db8:85a3:0000:0000:8a2e:0370:7334

Here are some important pointers for IPv6 addresses:
1) There are 8 segments in total.
2) Each segment has 4 hexadecimal digits. For example, 2001
3) Each hexadecimal digit is comprised of 4 bits. For example, 2001 will have 2 will be broken down to 0010, 0 will be 0000 and 1 will be 0001. So, 2001 will be written as <u>0010</u> <u>0000</u> <u>0000</u> <u>0001</u>

IPv6 addresses are long addresses, and they are not very easy to remember. There are some rules introduced to keep them a bit short and easy to write. Here are some of these rules:

1) 0000:0000 can be written as "::". It can only be used once in an address to avoid ambiguity. For example, "2001:0000:0000:0000:0000:0000:0000:abcd" can be shortened to "2001::abcd".
2) 0000 can be written as "0"
3) Leading Zeros: Leading zeros within a group of four hexadecimal digits can be omitted. For example, "2001:0db8" can be written as "2001:db8".
4) IPv4-Compatible IPv6 Addresses: IPv4 addresses can be represented within an IPv6 address using the notation "::ffff:w.x.y.z", where "w.x.y.z" is the IPv4 address. The "::ffff:0:192.0.2.1" can be written as "::ffff:c000:201".
5) IPv6 Link-Local Addresses: Link-local addresses, which are used for communication within a single

network segment, can be represented by starting with the prefix "fe80::". The interface identifier (last 64 bits) is typically derived from the MAC address of the network interface, but it can also be randomly generated.

Here are some more fun facts about IPv6 addresses:

1) Multicast IPv6 addresses start with the prefix "ff00::/8"
2) The loopback address in IPv6 is "::1", which is equivalent to the IPv4 loopback address (127.0.0.1). It is used for testing and communication with the local host.
3) Multicast address "ff02::1" is the "All Nodes" multicast address, used to send packets to all nodes on the local network segment. Similarly, "ff02::2" is the "All Routers" multicast address, used to send packets to all routers on the local network segment.

Address Resolution Protocol

Address resolution protocol is a protocol used to discover the MAC address associated with an IP address.

Reverse Address Resolution Protocol

Reverse address resolution protocol is a protocol used by a computer networking device to request an IP address. A host device sends its MAC or Physical address to the RARP server. RARP server maintains the mappings of specific MAC addresses to their respective IP addresses.

Dynamic Host Configuration Protocol

DHCP is a protocol that facilitates a DHCP server to automatically provide the IP address, subnet mask, and default gateway to its clients. Routers can also be used as DHCP servers. You may think for a moment, what's the big deal about this? I remember my first job as a network administrator. There were about 110 computers in that environment running Microsoft Windows and I was using static IP addresses. It was very tedious to manage that, and I had to maintain a list of used IP addresses. Now when I look back, I can't even imagine implementing this static IP configuration in an environment of thousands of computers on a single network.

Domain Name System

DNS is used to map domain names with IP addresses. This helps us in providing easy to remember domain names. A DNS server keeps track of domain names and IP addresses. When you try to go to juniper.net, it is your DNS server that provides the correct IP address of the website to ensure that your request reaches the correct domain. Remember,
network devices understand IP addresses, not the domain names.

Network Address Translation (NAT)

Network Address Translation (NAT) is used to translate private IP addresses to valid WAN (Wide Area Network) IP addresses. For example, if you have a webserver on your network with a private IP address of 192.168.1.10, you cannot access this server over the internet. So, if you want to access this server over the internet, you must use a valid WAN IP address provided by your Internet Service Provider. WAN IP addresses are limited in number and service providers charge a monthly fee to provide you a designated WAN IP. This type of NAT is called static NAT, and it provides One-To-One translation.

Port Address Translation (PAT)

Let's expand on the above concept of NAT. Now, imagine you have five different servers using Private IP addresses. If you want to access these servers over the internet, you must have one valid WAN IP address per server. This means you will have to pay for five WAN IP addresses to access these five servers over the internet. However, with PAT you can use one valid WAN IP address to translate multiple private IP addresses. So, in this scenario, we can use one WAN IP to translate five private addresses. PAT facilitates One-To-Many address translation. If instead of five servers, we have fifty servers using PAT, the network will not scale well. It will be slow and clunky. This problem can be resolved by dynamic network address translation.

Dynamic Network Address Translation

Dynamic NAT dynamically assigns public IP addresses from a pool of available addresses to private IP addresses on an as-needed basis. The mappings are typically temporary and released after a certain period of inactivity.

Core Distribution and Access

"Core distribution access" is a very commonly used network architecture design. Here are the three layers explained in a bit more detail.

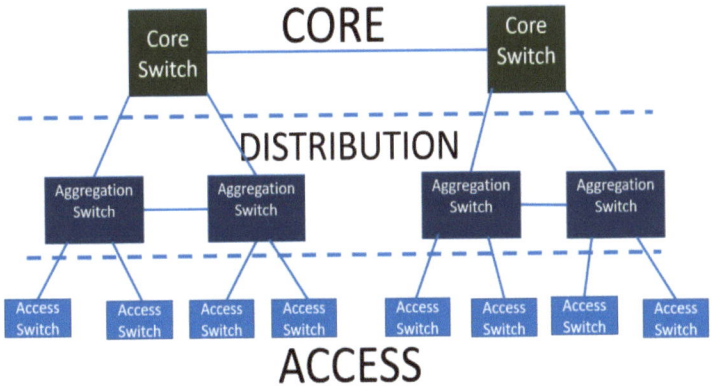

Core Layer

The core layer is the backbone of the network and handles high-speed, high-capacity traffic routing. Its primary function is to provide fast and efficient data forwarding between different distribution points or core switches.

Distribution Layer

The distribution layer acts as an intermediary between the core and access layers. Its primary role is to aggregate and distribute network traffic from the access layer to the core layer. The distribution layer performs functions such as policy enforcement, access control, and routing between different VLANs (Virtual Local Area Networks). It may also provide redundancy and load balancing for improved network performance and reliability.

Access Layer:

The access layer is the closest to end-user devices such as computers, printers, and IP phones. It provides network connectivity for these devices and typically consists of switches or access points. The access layer is responsible for connecting end-user devices to the distribution layer and implementing policies and security measures at the edge of the network.

Leaf and Spine

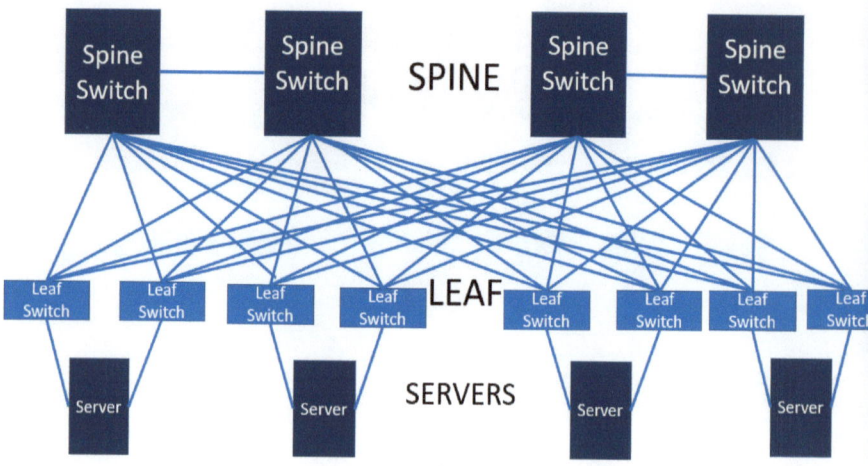

"Leaf and spine" network architecture design is commonly used in data centers to provide high-performance and scalable network connectivity. It is also known as Clos network. It was named after an American engineer Charles Clos.

In a leaf and spine architecture, the network is organized into two types of switches: leaf switches and spine switches.

Leaf Switches

Leaf switches are the access switches that directly connect to end-user devices, servers, and storage systems in the data center. They serve as the entry point for traffic coming into and going out of the data center. Leaf switches typically have a large number of ports and provide high-bandwidth connectivity to the devices connected to them.

Spine Switches

Spine switches are the backbone switches that interconnect the leaf switches in a non-blocking, full-mesh topology. They form multiple parallel paths between the leaf switches, providing high-speed and low-latency communication between any leaf switch pair. Spine switches have a high port density to accommodate the connections from multiple leaf switches.

The leaf and spine architecture offers several advantages.

Scalability

It provides a scalable solution as the network can easily accommodate additional leaf switches without impacting performance. The full-mesh connectivity between spine switches and leaf switches allows for linear scalability.

High Bandwidth

With the leaf and spine design, there are multiple paths for traffic to travel, resulting in high bandwidth and reduced congestion. This architecture ensures that network traffic can be distributed evenly across multiple links.

Low Latency

The direct and equal-distance connectivity between leaf and spine switches minimizes the latency in data transmission. This is particularly important in data center environments where low-latency communication is crucial for applications and services.

Redundancy

The leaf and spine architecture provides built-in redundancy. If a link or switch fails, alternate paths are available to ensure uninterrupted connectivity between leaf switches.

Overall, the leaf and spine architecture offers a scalable, high-performance, and resilient network solution for data centers, making it suitable for modern data-intensive applications and cloud environments.

1) Secure shell (SSH) uses TCP service port 22.
2) Telnet uses TCP service port 23.
3) FTP uses TCP service port 21. FTP uses port 21 for the control channel and port 20 for the data.
4) SMTP (Simple Mail Transport) uses TCP service port 25.
5) DNS uses both UDP and TCP port 53.
6) OSI model has seven layers. Layer 1 to 7 – Physical Layer, Data Link Layer, Network Layer, Transport Layer, Session Layer, Presentation Layer and Application Layer.
7) DOD Model has Network Layer, Internet Layer, Transport Layer and Application Layer.
8) ARP (Address Resolution Protocol) is a communication protocol that maps a network address (IP Address) to a physical address (MAC address).

2 Switching

Switching technology works on layer two of OSI model. This is a very important component of local area networks. Switching is faster and switch ports are cheaper in cost as compared to routing ports. In old times, switches used to be very expensive. Networks used to have hubs.

Network Hub

A hub is a networking device that operates at the physical layer of the OSI model. A hub network is a big collision domain. In a hub network, all devices listen to all the data traversing on the network segment. So, security and efficiency are major concerns for such networks. Hubs are largely obsolete and have been replaced by switches in modern networks.

Network Switches

Network switches are layer two devices. Every switch port creates a collision domain. A network with multiple switches is a big broadcast domain. Switches are very popular devices in enterprise environments. A switch is used in a LAN (Local Area Network) to add more devices to the same network. A switch can also be used to extend LAN capabilities in a large campus network. In such scenarios, a switch is connected to another switch to extend the existing local area network. The switched network creates a big broadcast domain and that can slow down the network. A broadcast domain is open to all the switches in the domain, so it is not a very scalable and secure solution.

As I mentioned earlier, a switched network with one big broadcast domain is not scalable due to a lack of efficiency and security. So, network engineers came up with a solution. A big broadcast domain was divided into multiple small broadcast domains. In the switching world, we call these broadcast domains VLANs. If a network consists of a big broadcast domain of fifty switches, we can divide it into smaller size domains of 10 switches per domain. This means that there will be 5 broadcasting domains and there will be 10 switches in each domain. In more technical language we say that a large switch network was divided into 5 different VLANs. VLANS are generally given a unique number or name to be identified on the network.

A single switch can have different ports assigned to different VLANs. A host in VLAN 2 cannot communicate with a host in VLAN 3 without a router. To communicate between two or more different VLANs we need a layer 3 device such as a router.

In an environment where VLANs are configured, a switch port can be configured as an access port or trunk port. An access port is a port that carries traffic from a specific VLAN.

A trunk port is a port that carries traffic from multiple VLANs.

Switch Port Stages

A switch port goes through different stages during its operation. Here are the typical stages:

Blocking:

When a switch port first becomes active, it goes into the blocking state. In this state, the port does not forward any data frames but listens to Bridge Protocol Data Units (BPDUs) to participate in the Spanning Tree Protocol (STP) negotiation. The blocking state helps prevent loops in the network before the STP determines the optimal path.

Listening

After the blocking state, the switch port transitions to the listening state. In this state, the port continues to listen to BPDUs and prepares to enter the learning state. It does not forward data frames in this state.

Learning

In the learning state, the switch port starts to learn MAC addresses by inspecting the source MAC addresses of received data frames. The switch updates its MAC address table with the port associated with each MAC address. However, the port still does not forward frames at this stage.

Forwarding

Once the learning state is complete, the switch port enters the forwarding state. In this state, the port actively forwards data frames between connected devices. It uses the MAC address table to determine the correct outgoing port for each frame based on its destination MAC address.

Disabled

If a switch port is administratively disabled or encounters an error, it may be in a disabled state. In this state, the port is completely inactive and does not participate in network operations.

These stages represent the typical behavior of a switch port during its operation, following the Spanning Tree Protocol's rules and participating in MAC address learning and forwarding.

Broadcast Storm

A broadcast storm is a phenomenon that can occur in a network when the broadcast or multicast packets are continually broadcast and forwarded by network devices, consuming excessive network bandwidth, and resulting in network congestion or even a complete network outage. This can happen when there is a switching loop, where frames are forwarded continuously between switches, leading to an exponential increase in the number of frames being transmitted. To prevent broadcast storms, network administrators use techniques such as spanning tree protocol (STP) to detect and disable loops or limit the amount of broadcast traffic in the network.

Spanning Tree Protocol

STP stands for Spanning Tree Protocol. This is a networking protocol that helps prevent loops in a switch. Switching loops can lead to broadcast storms and can deteriorate network performance. STP works by electing a root bridge, which serves as the root of the spanning tree, and then calculating the shortest path from each network device to the root. This path is then used to disable redundant links, effectively creating a loop-free network topology. STP is a standardized protocol and is widely used in Ethernet networks. There are several variations of STP, such as Rapid STP (RSTP) and Multiple STP (MSTP), which offer additional features and improvements over the original STP protocol.

Root Bridge

In a network that uses the Spanning Tree Protocol (STP), the root bridge is the designated bridge that serves as the reference point for all other bridges in the network. The root bridge is elected based on the bridge priority value. The bridge with the lowest priority becomes the root bridge. If multiple bridges have the same priority, then the bridge with the lowest MAC address is elected as the root bridge. All other bridges in the network maintain a record of the best path to the root bridge, and this information is used to determine which ports on each bridge should be put into forwarding or blocking mode to prevent network loops. The root bridge is an important concept in STP, as it serves as the basis for creating a loop-free network topology.

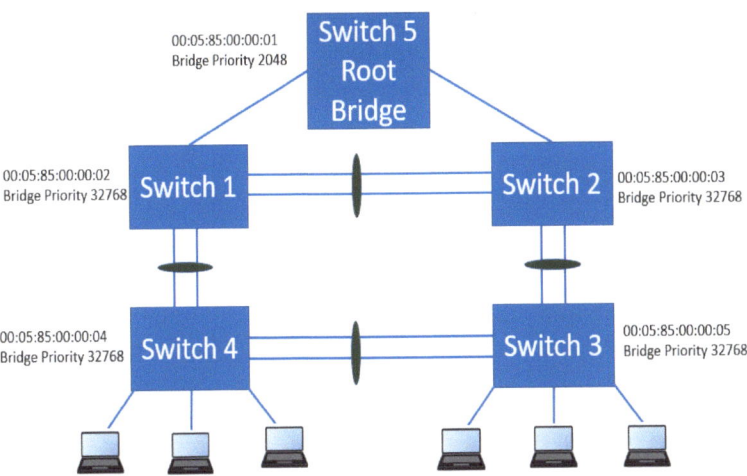

Let's discuss the root bridge election process based on the above topology. All switches have default bridge priority of 32768 except Switch 5 that has bridge priority of 2048. When it comes to bridge priorities, a lower number is preferred. So, in the above network topology Switch 5 will become root bridge. For some reason if switch 5 goes down, the switch with lowest bridge priority will become root bridge. In this case all other switches are configured with default bridge priority of 32768. So, in this case switch with lowest MAC address Switch 1 will become root bridge.

Port Channel (Cisco) or AE Bundle (Juniper)

A Port channel, also known as link aggregation or Ether Channel, is a networking technology that allows multiple physical links between switches or routers to be combined into a single logical link. This provides increased bandwidth, redundancy, and load-balancing capabilities. The multiple physical links are bundled together and appear as a single logical link to higher-layer network devices. This technology is supported by various networking vendors including two major players Cisco and Juniper. It uses various protocols for link aggregation, including Link Aggregation Control Protocol (LACP) and Port Aggregation Protocol (PAgP).

AE Bundle, short for Aggregated Ethernet Bundle, is a type of port aggregation technology used in Juniper Networks devices. It enables the bundling of multiple physical Ethernet links into a single logical interface. The AE bundle appears as a single interface to the network, providing increased bandwidth, redundancy, and load-balancing capabilities. It uses the Link Aggregation Control Protocol (LACP) to negotiate the bundle's configuration parameters, such as the number of links, the link speed, and the load-balancing algorithm. The AE bundle is commonly used in data centers, service provider networks, and other high-performance networking environments.

How does switching work?

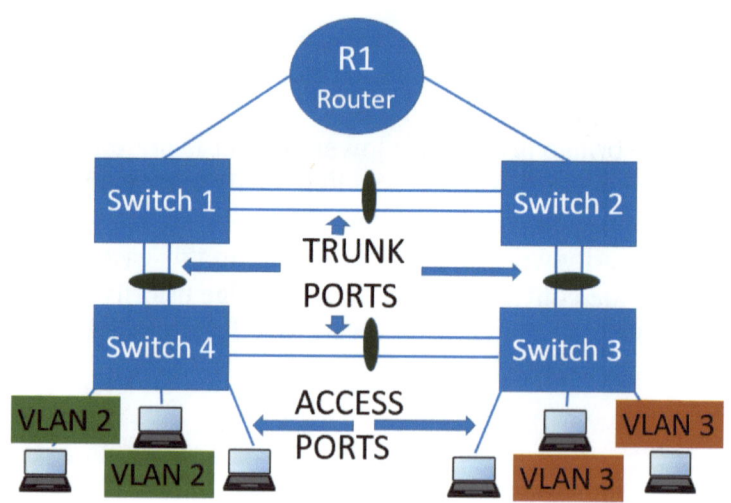

Now let us discuss this switch network. The ports which are connected to laptops and carry a specific VLAN traffic, are called access ports.

Switch ports connected to other switches are called trunk ports. Trunk ports carry multiple VLAN traffic. If a laptop connected to VLAN 2 has to communicate with a laptop connected to VLAN 3, it has to communicate via router. The router facilitates the routing of traffic between two different VLAN's.

1. A switch operates at the data link layer and forwards frames based on MAC addresses, while a hub operates at the physical layer and simply broadcasts all frames to all devices on the network.
2. A switch learns MAC addresses by examining the source MAC address of each incoming frame and associating it with the port on which the frame was received.
3. VLAN tagging is the process of adding a VLAN identifier to an Ethernet frame to indicate which VLAN the frame belongs to.
4. A static VLAN is manually configured on a switch, while a dynamic VLAN is assigned based on a device's MAC address or other criteria.
5. Virtual LANs (VLANs) provide a way to segment a network into smaller broadcast domains for security, performance, or organizational reasons.
6. LACP (Link Aggregation Control Protocol) allows multiple physical links between switches to be combined into a single logical link for increased bandwidth and redundancy.
7. Port security is a feature that allows a switch to limit the number of MAC addresses that can be learned on a particular port to prevent unauthorized devices from connecting to the network.
8. Cut-through switching forwards frames as soon as the destination MAC address is known, while store-and-forward switching buffers the entire frame and verifies its integrity before forwarding it.
9. EtherChannel allows multiple physical links between switches to be combined into a single logical link for increased bandwidth and redundancy.
10. RSTP reduces the convergence time of the Spanning Tree Protocol (STP) by enabling faster transition to the forwarding state.
11. A jumbo frame is an Ethernet frame with a larger payload size than the standard 1500 bytes, which can improve network performance by reducing overhead.

12. MAC address ageing is the process by which a switch removes inactive MAC addresses from its table to free up resources.
13. A MAC address table is a list of MAC addresses and their associated port on a switch.
14. A static ARP entry is manually configured on a device, while a dynamic ARP entry is automatically learned through ARP broadcasts.
15. A virtual switch is a software-based switch used in virtualization environments to connect virtual machines to a network.
16. A Layer 2 loop occurs when there are multiple paths between switches in a network, causing frames to be continuously forwarded in a loop and causing network congestion.
17. A static MAC address entry is manually configured on a switch, while a dynamic MAC address entry is learned automatically through incoming frames.
18. Port mirroring is a feature that copies all traffic from one or more ports on a switch to another port for monitoring or analysis purposes.
19. Spanning Tree Protocol (STP) is a Layer 2 protocol used to prevent Layer 2 loops and ensure a loop-free path in a network by disabling redundant paths.

20. A loop guard is a feature that helps prevent loops in a network by monitoring the state of ports and disabling ports that are suspected of causing loops.
21. A root guard is a feature that prevents a switch from becoming the root bridge of the network by blocking ports that receive superior BPDUs.
22. VRRP is a protocol used to provide redundancy for the default gateway by allowing multiple routers to share a virtual IP address.
23. HSRP is a Cisco proprietary protocol that provides similar functionality to VRRP but only allows for one active router at a time.
24. A Layer 2 firewall is a device that filters network traffic based on MAC addresses, VLANs, and other Layer 2 parameters.
25. VTP is a protocol that allows switches to share VLAN information automatically and synchronize VLAN

configurations across multiple switches.

26. A broadcast storm is a phenomenon that occurs when a large number of broadcast packets are generated and propagated through a network, causing congestion and degraded performance. It can be prevented by implementing Spanning Tree Protocol, loop guards, and other measures to prevent loops in the network. The root bridge is the central bridge in a Spanning Tree topology that all other bridges are connected to, while designated bridges are non-root bridges that have been selected to forward traffic for a particular segment.

3 Routing Basics

Routing is one of the most important inventions in the history of the Internet. Routing happens on layer three of the OSI model. So, obviously, routers are layer three devices. There are two types of routing:

> Static Routing
> Dynamic Routing

Static Routing

As the name suggests, it is manually configured on each router on the network. So as a network administrator, you need to know the available routers and routes on the network. Then you configure static routes on every single router on the network for the available destinations. This is not a very scalable solution for big networks.

Dynamic Routing

Dynamic routing protocols use algorithms to learn the network topology and to decide the best routes available to various destinations on a network. You can say that this is like automating the routing functionality. Dynamic protocols pretty much do the same job as what network engineers do in a static routing environment. There are two types of routing protocols:
> Distance Vector Protocol
> Link State Protocol

Distant Vector Protocols

Distance vector protocols make routing decisions based on hop counts.

Let's discuss this topology. In this example we are running a distant vector protocol and a data packet needs to go from router R1 to router R3. There are two routes available:

R1-R2-R3

R1-R3

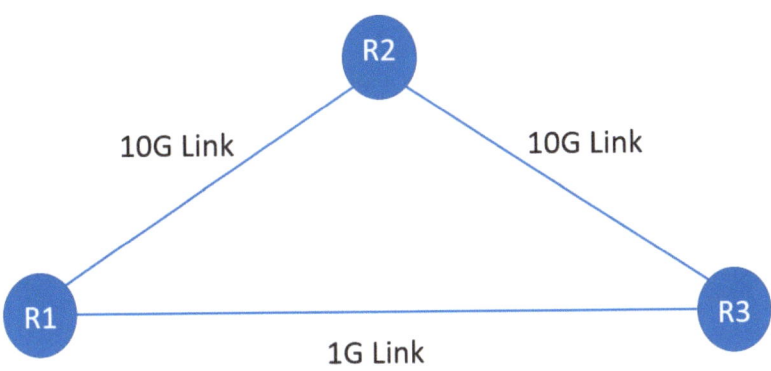

As you can see, in the first route there is one router in between the routers R1 and R3. If a data packet is traversing from R1 to R3, the packet must hop to router R2. There is one hop between the source and the destination. In the second route, a data packet from R1 will straight go to R3. There is no router in between. Distant vector protocol will prefer a route with the lowest hop count. So, in this case, R1-R3 will be the preferred route.

So why even bother with Link state protocols? Now have a closer look at the link speed for both routes. Route R1-R2-R3 is on a 10G link and route R1-R3 has a 1G link. Commonsense says that R1-R2-R3 is the best route, however distant vector algorithm does not have the intelligence to make that decision. The routing decisions are based on hop count so in this case a distant vector protocol will choose a slower link as the best path. RIPv1 and RIPv2 are examples of distant vector protocols.

Link State Protocols

Link state protocols have the intelligence to select the best routes based on the network topology. Link state protocols are also called the shortest path first. In the Link state routing environment, each router has the entire network map, and it calculates all possible routes to each destination and maintains the best route in a routing table. OSPF and ISIS are examples of link-state protocols.

Administrative Distance

Administrative distance is a unique numeric value assigned to routes and it is a measure of trustworthiness of a route. The lesser value administrative distance is preferred or more trustworthy. Let's say a route is configured as a static route and the same route is also learned via OSPF. The administrative distance for the static route is 1 and the administrative distance of OSPF is 110. So, in this case, the router will prefer the static route over the route learned via OSPF.

Routing Protocol	Administrative Distance
Directly Connected	0
Static Route out to an Interface	0
Static Route to next hop	1
EIGRP Summary Route	5
External BGP	20
Internal EIGRP	90
IGRP	100
OSPF	110
IS-IS	115
RIP	120
EGP	140
External EIGRP	170
Internal BGP	200
Unknown	255

1) A routing table is a database that contains information about how to forward data packets between different networks. It includes entries for each network, which specify the best path for packets to take to reach their destination.

2) A routing protocol is a set of rules that determine how routers communicate with each other to exchange information about network topology and determine the best path for data packets to take.

3) A default gateway is the router on a network that is used to forward data packets to other networks or the Internet when a specific route is not defined in the routing table.

4) Static routing is a type of routing where the network administrator manually configures the routing table entries for each network, rather than relying on a routing protocol to automatically determine the best path.

5) Dynamic routing is a type of routing where routers use a routing protocol to exchange information and automatically update their routing tables to determine the best path for data packets to take.

6) A hop count is the number of routers that a data packet must pass through to reach its destination. Each time a packet is forwarded to another router, the hop count is incremented by one.

7) A subnet is a smaller network within a larger network. It is created by dividing the IP address space of the larger network into smaller ranges.

8) A subnet mask is a 32-bit number that is used to identify the network and host portions of an IP address. It is used in conjunction with the IP address to determine the network and host addresses for a particular network.

9) A default route is a route that is used by a router to forward data packets to other networks or to the Internet when no other route is available in the routing table. It is often set to the IP address of the router's default

gateway.

10) A routing loop is a situation where data packets are continually forwarded between two or more routers, without ever reaching their destination. This can occur when there is a misconfiguration in the routing tables, causing the routers to continually forward the packets to each other.

11) A metric is a value used to measure the desirability of a particular route. It is used by routing protocols to determine the best path for data packets to take. Metrics can include factors such as bandwidth, delay, cost, and reliability.

12) Static routing involves manually configuring the routing table on each router, while dynamic routing uses a routing protocol to automatically determine the best path for data packets to take. Static routing is simpler to configure but may not be as efficient or adaptable as dynamic routing.

13) IGPs are used to exchange routing information within a single autonomous system (AS), while EGPs are used to exchange routing information between different autonomous systems. Examples of IGPs include RIP, OSPF, and EIGRP, while BGP is an example of an EGP.

14) A link-state routing protocol is a type of routing protocol that exchanges information about the entire network topology between routers. Each router builds a complete map of the network and uses this information to determine the best path for data packets to take. Examples of link-state routing protocols include OSPF and IS-IS.

15) A distance-vector routing protocol is a type of routing protocol that exchanges information about the distance and direction to other networks. Each router maintains a routing table that contains information about the distance and direction to each network and uses this information to determine the best path for data packets to take. Examples of distance-vector routing protocols include RIP and BGP.

16) Routing is the process of forwarding data packets between different networks or subnetworks, while

switching is the process of forwarding data packets within a single network. Switching is typically faster and simpler than routing, since it does not involve the complex decision-making processes required for routing.

4 Open Shortest Path First

OSPF stands for open shortest path first. This is a routing protocol for IP networks. It uses a link state routing algorithm and falls into the group of interior gateway protocols (IGP). OSPF Version 2 is for IPv4 and OSPF Version 3 is for IPv6 route prefixes. OSPF has an administrative distance of 110.

OSPF Areas

An OSPF area is a collection of multiple routers in contiguous networks in a single autonomous system. A unique Area ID is assigned to router interfaces residing in the same area. A router can be part of multiple areas. In OSPF a single autonomous system can be divided into multiple areas. Area 0 is called the backbone area. To have complete connectivity via OSPF, all other areas should be directly connected to the backbone area.

Three main reasons to implement OSPF

It decreases routing overhead.
It speeds up convergence.
It confines network instability to single areas of networks.

OSPF default timers

Hello timer is the duration at which a routing protocol sends hello packets to its neighbors. OSPF has a hello interval of 10 seconds which means that an OSPF router sends hello packets to its neighbors every 10 seconds.
Dead interval is the amount of time a router will wait without receiving a hello packet from a neighbor before declaring it dead. OSPF dead interval is 40 seconds. This is four times the

hello timer. It means that if an OSPF router does not receive a Hello packet from a neighbor for 40 seconds, it considers the OSPF neighbor as unreachable.

Link State Advertisements

OSPF uses LSAs to communicate its routing information to other OSPF routers.

LSA Retransmission Interval

The link-state advertisement (LSA) retransmission interval optimizes the sending and receiving of LSA and acknowledgment packets. You must configure the LSA retransmission interval to be equal to or greater than 3 seconds to avoid triggering a retransmit trap because the Junos OS delays LSA acknowledgments by up to 2 seconds. If you have a virtual link, you might find an increased performance by increasing the value of the LSA retransmission interval.

OSPF Configuration Components

OSPF has five configuration components that must match for an OSPF neighborship to establish; these include:

The OSPF neighbors must be in the same area.
The OSPF neighbors must have the same authentication configuration.
The OSPF neighbors must be on the same subnet.
The OSPF neighbors' hello and dead intervals must match.
The OSPF neighbors must have matching stub flags.

Router ID

OSPF uses Router ID for identifying a router uniquely in an OSPF network. OSPF chooses the highest IP address of all configured loopback interfaces as the Router ID. If no loopback interface is configured, then the highest IP address of the active physical interface is chosen by OSPF. The Designated Router (DR) DR is elected when OSPF routers are connected to the broadcast domain.

Router Priority

The router priority is a value assigned to each OSPF router. The default priority is 1. Routers with higher priority values have a greater chance of becoming the DR or BDR. If a router's priority is set to 0, it is ineligible to become the DR or BDR. This can be useful when you want to prevent a particular router from assuming those roles.

DR Election Process

OSPF router with the highest priority becomes DR. If there is a tie due to the same priority, the highest Router ID wins. Backup Designated Router (BDR) is a hot standby for DR. This means if DR goes down for some reason, BDR becomes the designated router.

Area Border Router (ABR)

Area Border Router or ABR is a router that has a presence in multiple areas of OSPF. In simple words, an ABR router connects two or more OSPF areas.

Autonomous System Border Router (ASBR)

Autonomous System Border Router or ASBR is an OSPF router that is connected to an external autonomous system via BGP.

OSPF multicast addresses

All OSPF routers use multicast address 224.0.0.5 to send hello packets. The designated router uses multicast address 224.0.0.6.

Topological Database

The topological database has information from all the link state advertisements. The topological database is input to the Dijkstra algorithm for computing the shortest path.

OSPF Network Topologies

There are four different kinds of OSPF topologies:

Broadcast multi-access
Non-broadcast multi-access
Point-to-Point
Point-to-multipoint

Broadcast and point-to-point networks send hello every 10 seconds.
Non-broadcast and point-to-multipoint sends hello every 30 seconds

OSPF Metrics

OSPF metric is used to prioritize one route over the other going to the same destination. Lower metric cost is preferred. For example, if there are two routing paths available with metric 200 and 300, the preferred route will be the one with metric 200.

When OSPF routers communicate with each other, they go through several states to establish an adjacency and exchange information. The different states of OSPF adjacency formation are discussed in the next section.

OSPF Seven States

Down State

In this state, the router has not yet detected a neighboring router and has not started the adjacency process.

Init State

In this state, the router has detected a neighboring router and has sent a hello packet to it. The router is waiting for a hello packet in response.

Two-Way State

In this state, the router has received a hello packet from the neighboring router and has sent a hello packet in response. The routers have exchanged enough information to establish bi-directional communication.

ExStart State

In this state, the routers are negotiating the terms of the adjacency, including the initial sequence number.

Exchange State

In this state, the routers are exchanging information about their link-state databases. Each router sends a link-state request to the other and responds with a link-state update.

Loading State

In this state, the routers are exchanging large amounts of information about their link-state databases. The routers send link-state requests and updates until they have exchanged all the necessary information.

Full State

In this state, the routers have completed the adjacency process and have exchanged all the necessary information about their link-state databases. The routers are now ready to participate in the OSPF routing process.

OSPF LSA Types

LSA Type 1: Router LSA is Router information sent by all routers.

LSA Type 2: Network LSA is Network information sent by a designated router.

LSA Type 3: Summary LSA carries Inter Area information, and it is sent by ABR.

LSA Type 4: Summary ASBR LSA is ASBR Information Sent by ABR.

LSA Type 5: Autonomous system external LSA is external info sent by ASBR. Type 5 will get you to an external network.

LSA Type 6: Multicast OSPF LSA.

LSA Type 7: Not-so-stubby area LSA is External Network Information Sent by NSSA ASBR.

Stub Area

A stub area is an OSPF area that does not receive external routing information, i.e., it does not receive routes from networks outside of its own area. This is useful in situations where there are many routers and networks in an OSPF domain, and it is not necessary for every area to have access to external routing information.

Totally Stub Area

In a totally stub area, not only are external routes summarized, but so are all inter-area routes, resulting in only a single default route being advertised within the stub area. This can be useful in situations where there are many routers and networks within the OSPF domain, and the number of routes being exchanged needs to be minimized.

A stubby area is created to reduce the LSA database. It eliminates Type 5 LSA's or external LSA's (Autonomous system) and Type 3 LSA's or Inter-Area routes. ABR stops generating Type 3 LSAs. This means the default route helps in reachability. The injection of a default Type 3 LSA from the ABR is critical to the operation of a totally stubby area.

Not So Stubby Area

A not-so-stubby area is required when you connect your network to an external partner network. To have an ASBR in Not So Stubby Area allows for the injection of external routing knowledge by an ASBR using an NSSA external LSA Type 7

NSSA Type 1

In this type of NSSA, the ABR generates a Type 7 LSA for each external route and floods it throughout the NSSA. The DR in the NSSA translates these LSAs into Type 5 LSAs and floods them throughout the rest of the OSPF domain.

NSSA Type 2

In this type of NSSA, the ABR generates a single Type 7 LSA that summarizes all external routes and floods it throughout the NSSA. The DR in the NSSA translates this LSA into a Type 5 LSA and floods it throughout the rest of the OSPF domain.

How OSPF Works in a Network?

OSPF is a link state interior gateway protocol. An OSPF autonomous system can be divided into multiple areas. This eases the administration of large networks. All areas are connected to the backbone area also known as area zero. If an area is not directly connected to the backbone area, we can use virtual links to connect to the backbone area. In the OSPF domain, if there is a routing change, it is communicated to all the neighbors. This makes this protocol very chatty.
There are several ways to fine-tune and reduce the link state database. To reduce the LSA database we can configure stub areas or totally stubby areas. There is one more confusing term, "Not so stubby area". I know as if the stub area and the totally stub areas were not enough. Not-so-stubby areas (NSSA} are used to connect to external networks. Link state advertisements are the messages which OSPF uses to keep the routing information consistent on all the routers. There is a very easy way to remember these LSAs. Start thinking from a smaller unit and start building on it. As you know, in our solar system, we can start from the smallest entity which can be an atom and we can expand all the way to galaxies. Similarly, let's expand on the OSPF router, here is the order, OSPF router itself, then comes Network, subsequently we have area border router ABR that connects multiple areas and finally we have autonomous system border router ASBR, which connects to external networks. So, Type 1 LSA is Router LSA, and it is sent by all OSPF routers. Type 2 LSA is Network LSA sent by DR. Type 3 is a summary LSA sent by ABR. Type 4 is external ASBR

information sent by ABR. Type 5 is external network information sent by ASBR. Type 6 is multicast OSPF LSA. LSA Type 7 is very interesting. This is sent by NSSA ASBR, yes, it is a not so stubby area autonomous system border router. So, Type 7 is only generated in NSSA. As soon as Type 7 crosses ABR, Type 7 is turned into Type 5. To reduce LSA advertisements OSPF uses designated routers and backup designated routers. In an OSPF broadcast network, DR and BDR keep track of all the changes. So, if an OSPF router experiences any network changes, it communicates its network changes to DR and BDR. Then DR communicates these changes to the rest of the OSPF network. This drastically reduces the routing update chatter within the network. DR and BDR election process is another important aspect of the OSPF story. BDR is elected first and then DR is elected. We can configure a priority on the router to make it a DR or BDR. A router with the

highest priority becomes a designated router. If priority is not configured, then a router with the highest router-id becomes DR. OSPF algorithm has a distinct way to select router-id. The highest loopback IP address becomes a router-id. If for some reason a router does not have a loopback address, then the highest IP address on a router interface becomes router-id. This section summarizes and ties together all the concepts we have discussed so far. This is not a deep dive into the protocol. To have a better understanding of OSPF, you still need to read a textbook and you must work in the lab. However, the idea of this book is to refresh your basic knowledge and advanced concepts pertaining to OSPF.

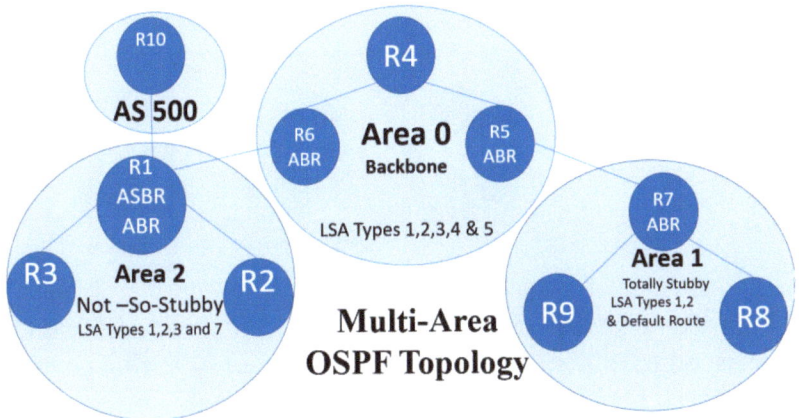

This is a network topology of an OSPF network. This is how Area 0 or the backbone area is connected to other areas. In Area 0, Router R5 is connected to Area 1 via Router R7. Router R6 in Area 0 is connected to Area 2 via Router R1. That's why R1, R6, R5 and R7 are Area Border Router (ABR). Router R1 in Area 2 is connected to an external autonomous system, that's why R1 is called ASBR.

OSPF on Broadcast Network Topology

OSPF Link State Advertisements (LSAs) are flooded to all routers in multi-access networks. The DR and BDR are elected in multi-access networks (such as Ethernet LANs) to reduce the amount of OSPF traffic and processing overhead on the network.

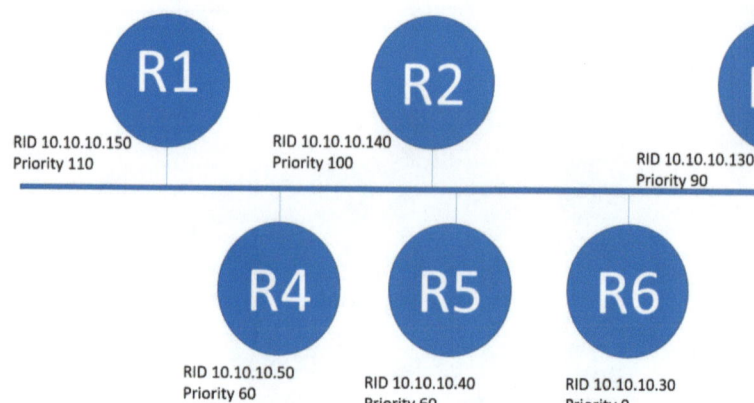

In this type of network, every router must be fully adjacent to every other router, which means that they must exchange their LSAs. To prevent every router from flooding its LSAs to every other router, the DR and BDR are elected to act as a hub between the other routers in the network.

When a router generates an LSA, it floods it to the DR and BDR first, if they are present. The DR and BDR then forward the LSA to all other routers in the network. If there is no DR or BDR in the network, then the router floods the LSA directly to all other routers.

The router with the highest OSPF priority on the network becomes the DR, and the router with the second-highest priority becomes the BDR. So, in the above topology router R1 is DR and router R2 is BDR.

If multiple routers have the same highest priority value, the router with the highest OSPF router ID becomes the DR, and the router with the next highest OSPF router ID becomes the BDR.

It is important to note that the DR and BDR election process only occurs on multi-access networks, where multiple routers are connected to the same network segment. In point-to-point networks, there is no need for a DR or BDR, and each router forms a point-to-point adjacency with the other router.

1) OSPF is a link-state interior gateway routing protocol and is open standard or vendor independent.

2) All OSPF routers in a broadcast network are neighbors because they exchange hello packets with each other.

3) An OSPF router is called adjacent if it has exchanged hello packets and LSAs.

4) Metric of OSPF is called cost and it is calculated using the formula 100/Interface Bandwidth (In Mbps).

5) OSPF router-id is a 32-bit number and is used to identify each router in the OSPF domain.

6) In the OSPF domain each router sends an update to all routers whenever there is a change in topology. The idea behind DR/BDR is that only DR/BDR can send any update to all routers.

7) BDR is elected prior to the DR.

8) OSPF algorithm has a specific way to select Router ID. The OSPF Router ID selection algorithm works as below: Any Manually configured OSPF Router ID in OSPF Process is selected as the OSPF Router ID. If there is no OSPF Router ID configured, then the Highest IP address on any Loopback Interfaces of the router is selected as the OSPF Router ID. If there are no Loopback Interfaces configured, the highest IP address on its active physical interfaces is selected as the OSPF Router ID.

9) OSPF supports Plain Text and MD5 authentications.

10) OSPF requires that the backbone area (area 0) must be connected to all other areas through an ABR. However, in some topologies, an OSPF area might not have a direct connection to the backbone area. In such cases, OSPF uses the virtual link to connect such an area the to backbone area virtually.

11) OSPF network types are Broadcast, Non-Broadcast multiple access (NBMA), Point-to-Point, Point-to-Multi-Point, and Point-to-Multi-Point Non-Broadcast.

12) OSPF router types are Internal Routers, Backbone Routers, ABR, and ASBR.

5 Intermediate System to Intermediate System

ISIS

ISIS stands for Intermediate System to Intermediate System. ISIS is an interior gateway protocol that uses link state information for routing decision. It is not based on IP. ISIS is based on CLNS (connectionless network services). ISIS is called integrated ISIS if it is supporting IP.
ISIS has an administrative distance of 115.

NET (Network Entity Title) Address

NETs take several forms, depending on your network requirements. NET addresses are hexadecimal and range from 8 octets to 20 octets in length. There are three major parts to the address structure: area, system ID, and N-selector. In these three parts Area comprises of Authority and Format Identifier (AFI) and Area ID.
A typical NET address looks like this 49.0001.1921.6800.1001.00. It consists of the following parts:

- 49—AFI authority and format Identifier

- 0001—Area ID

- 1921.6800.1001—System identifier

  The system identifier must be unique within the network. To keep this number unique this number is derived from the IP address. So, for example, 192.168.1.2 can be written as 192.168.001.002. Now the previous number is regrouped into four numbers separated by a dot 1921.6800.1002. Isn't it straightforward and simple?

- 00—Selector

The following ISO addresses illustrate the IS-IS address format:
49.0001.00a0.c96b.c490.00
49.0001.2081.9716.9018.00

ISIS Adjacency States

In the real world when two people want to exchange their ideas, they need to agree on common communication rules and a common language that they use and understand. Routers are not any different. Two routers running ISIS must establish adjacency before they can exchange routing information. Initial communication starts with hello messages. Here are different states of ISIS adjacencies:

New adjacency starts when ISIS is configured on the router.
One-Way adjacency state occurs when ISIS router sends a hello PDU
Initializing adjacency state is the state when an ISIS router receives a hello PDU from neighbor with its own information.
Up state of ISIS adjacency is the state when neighbor adjacency is established, and routing information is exchanged.
Down state of ISIS adjacency can result from a down physical interface, IP address mismatch, ISO area mismatch, expired hold timer, or a bad hello PDU.
Reject state is the result of an authentication mismatch. This state will finally get to down state.

ISIS Neighbor Adjacency Requirements

To establish ISIS adjacency successfully following parameters must match:

Hello packet format (Point-To-Point or Broadcast)
Hello timers
Router level (L1,L2,L1-L2)
Area (For L1 adjacency)
Authentication
MTU configured on interface

ISIS is a very popular IGP among internet service providers. ISIS protocol routing information can be categorized into two levels, Level 1 and Level 2. An ISIS network can be divided into multiple domains which are known as areas. This helps in administering the large ISIS networks efficiently. An ISIS router can be:

> Level 1 router
> Level 2 router
> Level 1/Level 2 (L1/L2) router

Level 1 router

Level 1 routers share intra-area information. This is the routing information pertaining to the same area.

Level 2 router

Level 2 routers share interarea information. This is the routing information between multiple areas. Level 2 routers are also called backbone routers.

Level 1/Level 2 router

ISIS Routers which connect multiple areas are called L1/L2 routers.

Designated Intermediate System (DIS)

DIS is also called pseudo node and it is very similar to a designated router in OSPF. It helps in reducing the amount of information that is generally exchanged between ISIS routers on a broadcast network. This facilitates faster SPF calculations and hence results in shorter convergence times. If N is the number of routers on a broadcast network, ISIS needs $N*(N-1)$ advertisements.

DIS election process is very simple. ISIS router with the highest DIS priority is elected as a DIS router or pseudo node. The default value of DIS priority in Juniper is 64. This ranges from 0 to 127. In case of a tie in DIS priorities between two routers, the highest MAC address wins.

How ISIS Works in a Network?

Here I will create a topology and explain how an ISIS protocol works in a network.

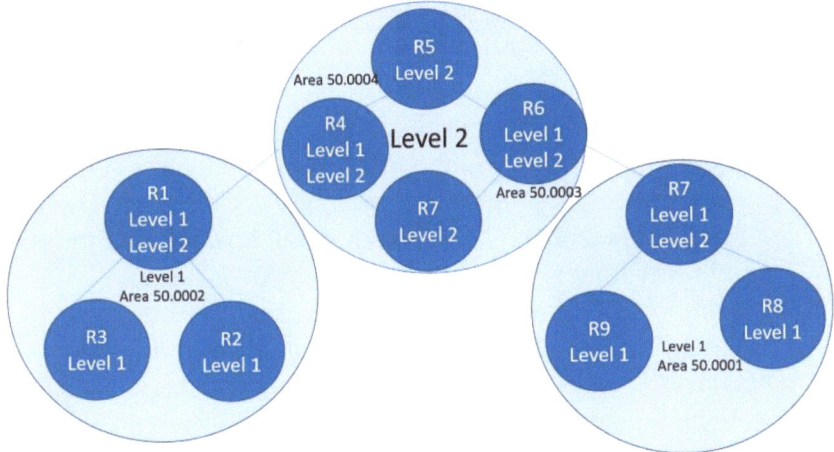

IS-IS is commonly used in large Service Provider and Enterprise networks and can be implemented in two different levels: Level 1 (L1) and Level 2 (L2).
IS-IS Level 1 is responsible for routing within an area, while IS-IS Level 2 is responsible for routing between different areas. IS-IS Level 1 routers communicate only with other routers within their own area, while IS-IS Level 2 routers communicate with other Level 2 routers both within their own area and in other areas.
In summary, IS-IS Level 1 is responsible for intra-area routing, while IS-IS Level 2 is responsible for inter-area routing. Both levels work together to provide efficient and scalable routing in large networks.

ISIS on a broadcast network

In Intermediate System to Intermediate System (IS-IS) networks, the Designated Intermediate System (DIS) is responsible for building and maintaining the Link State Database (LSDB) for a given network segment. The DIS router is elected through a process called DIS Election.

When a new router is added to a network segment or a router that was previously elected as DIS fails, a new DIS needs to be elected. The DIS election process is performed using a priority-based mechanism, where each router in the network segment has a priority value assigned to it. The router with the highest priority value is elected as the DIS.

If multiple routers have the same priority value, the router with the highest MAC address becomes the DIS. Once the DIS is elected, it is responsible for flooding the link state information to all other routers in the network segment.

It is important to note that the DIS election process occurs independently in each network segment within an IS-IS network. This means that multiple DISs can exist in a single IS-IS domain, with each DIS responsible for a different network segment.

In ISIS networks, the DIS is responsible for creating and maintaining the Link State Database (LSDB) for a given network segment.

The DIS is elected through a process called DIS Election.

The priority value is used to determine which router is selected as the DIS for a given network segment. Each router in the network segment has a priority value assigned to it, with higher priority values being preferred.

The default priority value for a router is 64, and the maximum value is 127. A higher priority value means that the router is more likely to be elected as the DIS.

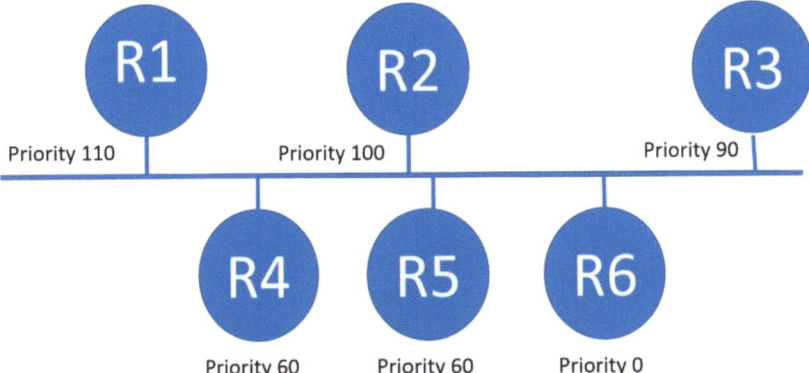

R1 is Designated Intermediate System (DIS) because it has the highest priority of 110.

R6 will never be elected as the DIS and it will not participate in the DIS election because priority is 0.

If multiple routers in the network segment have the same priority value, the router with the highest MAC address is selected as the DIS. This is because the MAC address is unique to each router and can be used as a tiebreaker in the DIS election process.

If a router is configured with a priority value of 0, it will never be elected as the DIS for any network segment. This is because a priority value of 0 indicates that the router is not eligible to be a DIS. In other words, the router will not participate in the DIS election process.

A router with a priority value of 0 will still participate in the network segment and form adjacencies with other routers, but it will not be selected as the DIS. Other routers in the network segment will elect a different router as the DIS based on their own priority values and the DIS election process.

Overall, configuring a router with a priority value of 0 can be useful in certain network scenarios where a router needs to participate in the network segment but should not be selected as the DIS.

So, here is a scenario where IS-IS routers are configured with the same priority.

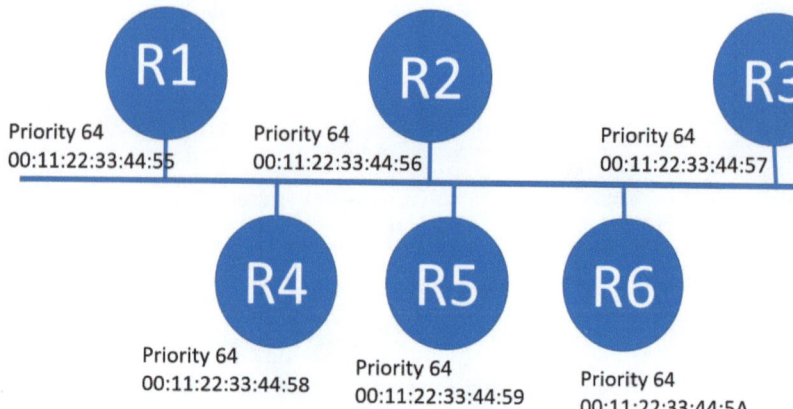

As you can see, all the above routers are configured with the same priority value of 64. R6 will be elected as the DIS because it has the highest MAC address. If there is a tie in priority values, the Router with the highest MAC address is elected as the DIS.

ISIS Interview Essentials

ISIS is a link state IGP (interior gateway protocol. It is very popular among internet service providers due to its scalability. Here are some facts about ISIS which are generally asked in interviews.

1. ISIS uses Dijkstra's algorithm for computing the best path through the network.
2. ISIS network is one autonomous system. ISIS routing domain comprises end systems (ES) connected via intermediate systems (IS)
3. SNPA (Sub-Network Point of Attachment) is the data-link address that facilitates reachability to a neighbor on broadcast media. An SNPA is generally a MAC address.
4. NET address is short for Network Entity Title. The NET address is a unique identifier for a router running ISIS. It is an NSAP, and it is 8 to 20 bytes long.
5. AFI (Authority and Format Identifier) of 0x47 is commonly used for global ISIS networks. AFI of 0x49

is used for private CLNP addresses and it cannot be routed globally.

6. CLNP is a connectionless network protocol and is very similar to IP. CLNP address is 20 bytes long and it resides on layer 3 of the OSI network model.

7. ISIS uses link-state packets (LSP) to advertise routing information to its neighbors.

8. ISIS uses an arbitrary cost for its metric. IS-IS additionally has three optional metrics: delay, expense, and error.

9. ISIS protocol has four types of protocol data units: Hello, LSP (Link State PDU), CSNP (Complete Sequence Number PDU), and PSNP (Partial Sequence Number PDU).

10. CSNP (Complete Sequence Number PDU) is an ISIS routing update that contains the full link state database. ISIS sends CSNP every 15 minutes.

11. L1 CSNP updates are sent to all Level-1 routers at a multicast address 01-80-C2-00-00-14.

12. L2 CSNP updates are sent to all Level-2 routers at a multicast address 01-80-C2-00-00-15.

13. PSNP (Partial Sequence Number PDU) carries partial LSPs. On a point-to-point network, PSNP is used to acknowledge received LSPs. On a broadcast network, PSNP is used to request the latest LSPs updates. Like CSNP, partial sequence number PDUs can be L1 or L2 (L1 PSNP or L2 PSNP)

14. ISIS protocol supports two types of topologies broadcast and point-to-point.

15. ISIS uses Link State PDU (LSPs) to distribute and exchange routing information. ISIS routers send LSP packets to collect and update routing information from ISIS neighbors. LSPs are used to establish and maintain adjacencies.

16. ISIS router with the highest priority will be elected as DIS. ISIS priority has a default value of 64. In case two ISIS routers have the same priority, the highest SNPA or MAC address will be elected as DIS.

17. ISIS sends hello packets every 10 seconds on a broadcast link. A designated intermediate system (DIS) sends a hello every 3.3 seconds.
18. ISIS has a default metric of 10.
19. LSP refresh interval timer is 900 seconds.
20. LSP transmission timer is 33 milliseconds.
21. In the case of larger networks core routers are added in Level 2 and smaller ISIS domains can be added in Level 1. L2 routers have complete knowledge of the network.

5 Border Gateway Protocol

BGP

BGP, Border gateway protocol is an exterior gateway routing protocol (EGP) that is used for routing between multiple autonomous systems. An Autonomous System (AS) is a collection of IP networks and routers managed by a single ISP. Autonomous systems are assigned unique identifiers called Autonomous System Numbers (ASNs) by regional Internet registries (RIRs). Internet service providers do connect to other internet service providers using BGP. To facilitate traffic from one ISP to another ISP, we need policy-based routing, that's nothing but border gateway protocol. BGP is a path vector protocol, and it sends routes with path information. BGP neighbors are manually configured. BGP sends updates to its neighbors as unicast.

BGP can also be used by organizations that have networks connected to multiple service providers. In other words, the multihoming of a router is possible due to BGP. A router that is connected to two different ISPs is called multihomed. BGP uses TCP Port 179.

BGP supports MD5 authentication. BGP is a policy-based protocol. Peer-Groups are helpful to apply similar policies to multiple neighbors. BGP is very handy for internet service providers because they may peer with several other ISPs or customers.

BGP Neighborship

A BGP router, while establishing a neighbor relationship, goes through the following stages:

Idle

This is the state when BGP is configured on a router for the very first time. In this state, a BGP router starts TCP sessions for its peers. All inbound sessions in this state are not accepted. Once a BGP router transitions from this state it starts looking for TCP sessions initiated by its BGP neighbors.

Connect

This is the state in which a BGP router completes a TCP session and transitions to an open state. If the TCP sessions fail because the neighbor is not reachable, the connect state transitions to the Active state. The ConnectRetry timer has a default value of 120 seconds. Once this timer reaches zero, the BGP router will make another attempt to complete the TCP session.

Active

In an active state, BGP router keeps trying to complete a TCP session. If a TCP session is complete, a BGP router sends an open message to its peer and transitions to opensent state. If for some reason a TCP session cannot be established, ConnectRetry timer will be reset to 120 again and another attempt will be made to complete the TCP session.

Open Sent

Once a TCP session is established BGP router transitions to opensent state. At this state a BGP router sends an opensent message and waits for an opensent message from a remote peer. As soon as an opensent message is received from BGP neighbor, the opensent state transitions to openconfirm.

Open Confirm

Open Confirm state comes into play when a BGP router receives open sent message and sends a keepalive message to its neighbor.

Established

This is the final and desirable state for BGP neighbors. This is the state that network engineers love to see. In opensent state, when a keepalive is sent and in response a keepalive is received back. At this point BGP neighbor relationship is established. BGP is an application layer protocol. It can be configured as IBGP or EBGP.

IBGP

IBGP is also called internal border gateway protocol. If a BGP session is established between two routers that belong to the same AS (autonomous system), it is called IBGP. IBGP has an administrative distance of 200.

EBGP

EBGP is also called external border gateway protocol. If a BGP session is established between two routers that belong to two different autonomous systems, it is called EBGP. EBGP has an administrative distance of 20.

BGP Use Cases

Here are some use cases where BGP is configured in the real world:

- Internet service providers use BGP for path manipulations.
- BGP is used in multihoming. This is a practice where organizations connect their local area networks with multiple service providers. Multihoming provides redundancy to the network, however, it costs extra dollars.
- BGP is also used for traffic path engineering.

EBGP Loop prevention mechanism

A router running EBGP in an autonomous system will not accept the same prefix that it is advertising to some other AS. In easy language, if a Router running BGP is advertising 10.20.30.0/24, it will not accept the same route from a router running BGP in some other autonomous system.

IBGP Loop prevention mechanism

A router running IBGP uses a split horizon to prevent loops. The BGP split-horizon rule states that a BGP router that receives a BGP route via an iBGP peering does not re-advertise that route to another router that is an iBGP peer. In short, a routing update sent by one IBGP neighbor to another should not be re-advertised to another IBGP neighbor. It is necessary to prevent routing loops.

So, because of the split horizon, to have complete route information, full mesh neighborships are required. This means all routers running IBGP must form neighborships with all other IBGP neighbors. So, inside an autonomous system, all IBGP peers should have a full mesh.

The inability of BGP to advertise a prefix learned from one IBGP peer to another IBGP peer can lead to scalability issues within an autonomous system. The formula $n(n-1)/2$ provides the number of BGP sessions required where n represents the number of routers in an autonomous system running BGP. For example, a full mesh topology of 5 routers requires 10 BGP sessions, and a topology of 10 routers requires 45 BGP sessions. IBGP scalability becomes an issue for large networks. This scalability issue can be addressed by configuring Route-Reflector or Confederations

Route reflectors

Route reflectors provide a scalable BGP solution for large networks. In the real world, a service provider can have hundreds of core routers. So, it is impractical to have full mesh topology on a BGP network. This can be accomplished by configuring a route reflector server and route reflector clients. As we have discussed in the earlier section IBGP routers do not readvertise the routing information that they learn from their IBGP peers. This mechanism is called split horizon and BGP uses this to avoid routing loops. When we configure a BGP router as a route reflector server it is exempted from the split horizon rule. This means that the route reflector server will learn BGP routes from IBGP routers which are configured as route reflector clients, and it readvertises what it learns from one route reflector client to another. This will help in reducing the overhead introduced by full mesh topology. In the real world, we have more than one route reflector servers to have some redundancy on the network. So, if one route reflector server fails others keep functioning. These route reflector servers can be fully or partially meshed based on the size of the network.

Confederations

Confederation is a BGP feature that facilitates us to split a large autonomous system into smaller autonomous systems. So, let's say we have an autonomous system that has a hundred routers running BGP. We can divide this large AS into smaller Sub-autonomous systems with 25 routers each. In this scenario, we have two options. We can have 25 BGP routers fully meshed, or we can configure route reflector servers and route reflector clients within these smaller sub-autonomous systems. These sub-autonomous systems are not visible to EBGP peers. EBGP peers see the BGP confederation network as one autonomous system.

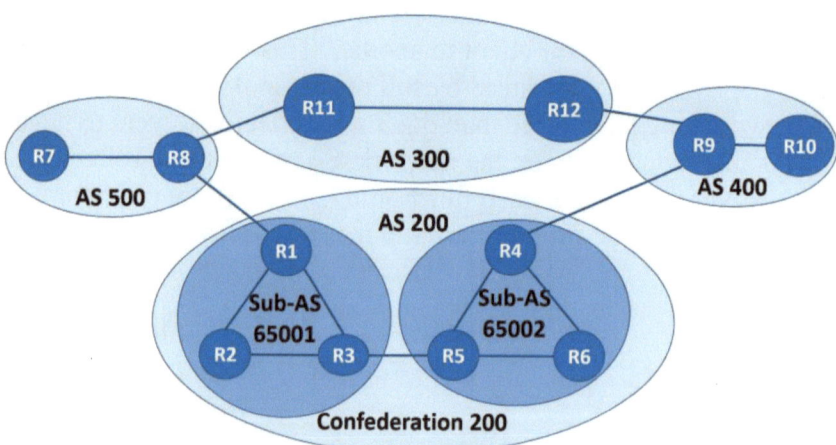

In the above network diagram AS 200 is divided into two sub-autonomous systems AS 65001 and 65002.

BGP Attributes

BGP chooses a route to a network based on the attributes.
There are two main categories of BGP attributes:
    Well-known attributes
    Optional attributes.

BGP Well-known attributes

Let's discuss well-known attributes of BGP in more detail. These well-known attributes have two categories:

Well-known mandatory
Well-known discretionary

Well-known mandatory attributes must be recognized by all BGP routers, present in all BGP updates, and passed on to other BGP routers. Well-known mandatory attributes are:
As path
Origin
Next hop

Well-known discretionary attributes must be recognized by all BGP routers and passed on to other BGP routers, but they need not be present in an update. For example, local preference is advertised to internal BGP peers but not to EBGP peers.

BGP optional attributes

Let's discuss BGP optional attributes in a bit more detail. BGP optional attributes have two categories:

Optional transitive
Optional non-transitive

Optional transitive might or might not be recognized by a BGP router, but it is passed on to other BGP routers. If not recognized, it is marked as partial. For example, Aggregator, community.

Optional non-transitive attributes are not advertised to BGP peers. If the BGP process does not recognize the attribute, then it can ignore the update and it does not advertise the path to its peers. For example, Multi-Exit Discriminator (MED), originator ID

This is all you need to know about BGP attributes at a high level. Some of the attributes are very important and they are used in the service provider industry on a day-to-day basis. If you are going to work for a service provider, you must dive deeply into the details of BGP attributes. Let's begin with well-known mandatory attributes.

Well-known mandatory

BGP well-known mandatory attributes must be present in BGP routing updates. Here is a list of these attributes:
AS Path
Next Hop
Origin

AS-PATH

AS Path information is used to decide on the best path. A route with the lowest number of AS hops is preferred.

Next-Hop

Next hop is another well-known mandatory attribute that must be sent along with BGP routing updates. When iBGP sends a routing update to another iBGP neighbor, it keeps the "next hop" the same. However, when eBGP sends a routing update to another eBGP neighbor, it changes the "next hop".
Here is a very common problem that arises in the networks based on this attribute. In case of an IBGP "next hop" stays the same and it can run into reachability issues. In Juniper and Cisco, we can configure next-hop-self. This changes the natural behavior of IBGP. As the command is self-explanatory, it changes the "next hop" to self before sending an IBGP routing update to the neighbor. This resolves the reachability issue.

Origin

Origin is an attribute that informs all AS in Internetwork how a network got introduced in BGP.

Well-known Discretionary

BGP has well-known discretionary attributes which are optionally included in its updates. These attributes are recognized by all BGP routers and are advertised to other BGP peers. Here are the two well-known discretionary:

Local Preference or Weight

Automatic Aggregate

Weight

Weight is an attribute that is Cisco proprietary. This helps BGP to decide on the best path when multiple paths are available to a destination. In other words, this attribute helps you to decide the exit point of the traffic, when multiple exit points are available for the same distance. A higher value is preferred, and it is local to the router. The default value is zero.

Local Preference

The local Preference attribute is used to determine the best exit path for an autonomous system. LOCAL_PREF is a BGP attribute used to control the outbound traffic path towards a destination that is on a different autonomous system and the destination has multiple redundant paths through multiple routers in an autonomous system. So, in simple words if a destination is reachable via AT&T and Verizon networks, as a telecommunication engineer you can decide which path to take to get to the destination.

Local-Preference with the higher value is preferred. This value decides how to exit an AS. The default value is 100. Local-Pref is advertised only to IBGP neighbors within an AS.

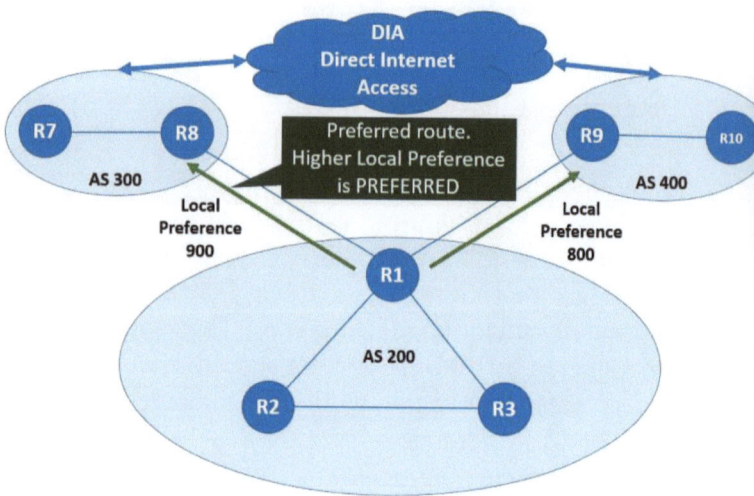

Let's discuss the above topology. We have AS 200 that is connected to AS 300 and AS 400 via router R1. Router R1 is called a multihomed router. As you can see in this scenario, we want to access the internet via AS 300, so this will be our primary route to internet access. The second route to the internet can be accessed via AS 400. This will be our backup route. To accomplish this, configuring local preferences comes in handy. Here, we set the local preference for the primary route as 900 and the local preference for the secondary route is set to 800. As we know that the highest value is preferred, so the route with a local preference of 900 will be preferred. If for some reason, this route goes down, traffic will be seamlessly moved to AS 400.

Optional transitive

Optional transitive BGP attributes might or might not be recognized by a BGP router, but it is advertised to other BGP peers. If a BGP router does not recognize an optional transitive attribute, it marks the attribute as partial. Here is the list of these attributes:

                Aggregator
                Community

Aggregator

Aggregator is an optional transitive attribute that is used to aggregate routing information from multiple BGP speakers into a single route. It is used in cases where a BGP speaker receives multiple routes from different peers for the same destination, and it needs to advertise a single route to other peers in its AS or in other autonomous systems.

An aggregator is a BGP attribute added by the router that performs route aggregation, and it includes the AS number and IP address of the router. This information is used by other BGP speakers to identify the router that performed the aggregation and to determine the best path to reach the aggregated route.

An aggregator is an optional attribute, which means that it may or may not be present in a BGP update message. If it is present, it is considered during the route selection process, but it does not affect the best path selection.

In summary, the aggregator is an optional transitive attribute that is used to aggregate routing information from multiple BGP speakers into a single route. It helps to reduce the size of the BGP table and improve the efficiency of the BGP routing system.

Community

Community is a BGP optional transitive attribute. A community attaches a tag to BGP routes. These tags help BGP in making routing decisions based on certain policies. This is the reason we call BGP a policy-based routing protocol. An ISP has multiple BGP peering sessions with customers and other service providers. Routes learned from the customers are treated differently as compared to routes learned from other peering partners (ISP's). So, in this case, ISP uses different communities for different service providers and customers. Think of it as a mechanism for tagging BGP routes.

Here are four BGP communities:
> Internet
> No-Advertise
> No-Export
> Local-AS

Optional non-transitive

These attributes may or may not be known to all BGP peers. If a BGP router receives an optional non-transitive attribute, the update should be advertised to peers without the unrecognized attributes. Here are optional non-transitive attributes:
> Multi-Exit Discriminator (MED)
> Originator
> Cluster ID

Multi-Exit Discriminator (MED)

MED is an optional and non-transitive BGP attribute. This attribute defines how traffic should enter an autonomous system. MED is advertised to EBGP neighbors only. It has a default value of zero. MED is also called metric in Cisco IOS. The lower value of MED is preferred over a high value. Don't get confused by the name Multi Exit Discriminator. You may think that this attribute controls the traffic exiting our autonomous system. However, this is not true. MED comes in handy when you have multiple routes to the same autonomous system. So, in a way you have multiple exits from your autonomous system going out. That's where the word "Multi-Exit" comes from. In the real world, an exit door can also be used to enter. The same is true in the routing world. BGP uses MED value to influence how traffic from a neighboring autonomous system will enter our autonomous system. When I use the word "Our autonomous system", I mean to say the autonomous system, that we are responsible for as network engineers. So always remember that MED decides how data traffic will enter our autonomous system.

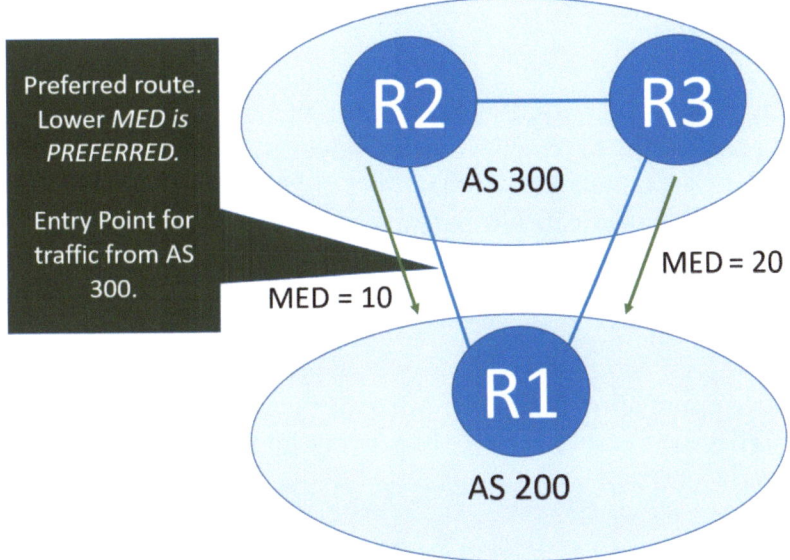

Let's discuss the above scenario. Imagine that you are a network engineer for AS 200. AS 300 is beyond your control. Technically network engineer on AS 300 can decide whether he wants to prefer R2-R1 link or R3-R1 link.

You as a network engineer for AS 200 can configure MED values on both the links. These MED values of 10 and 20 will be advertised along with BGP routing information to AS 300. So, if a router in AS 300 needs to send traffic to AS 200, it will select the link R2-R1, which has the lower MED value. So, by configuring a MED value you can influence the traffic entering your network when you have multiple exit points in your autonomous system.

Originator ID

BGP Originator ID is a BGP attribute that is used to prevent routing loops in BGP networks that have route reflectors. When a route reflector receives a route advertisement from one of its clients and then reflects that route to other clients, it sets the BGP Originator ID attribute to its own router ID. The Originator ID indicates the router that originated the route, which in this case is the route reflector.

The BGP Originator ID is useful in preventing routing loops because it allows the route reflector to identify and discard any reflected routes that have the same Originator ID as the route reflector itself.

This can occur if the route reflector receives a route from a client, reflects it to another client, and then receives the same route back from a different client.

By using the Originator ID, the route reflector can identify that the route was originally advertised by itself and can discard it to prevent routing loops.

It's important to note that the BGP Originator ID attribute is only used by route reflectors and is not a standard BGP attribute that is exchanged between all BGP routers.

Cluster ID

Cluster List is another attribute, that is nontransitive and is appended by the route reflector with its cluster-id. It is nothing but Route Reflector's BGP router ID. If a group of routers belongs to the same cluster, they will have the same cluster ID configured on them.

In a BGP network that uses Route Reflection, a route reflector is used to reflect BGP routes between iBGP peers. When a route reflector receives a BGP update from an iBGP peer, it reflects the update to other iBGP peers. In this scenario, the route reflector replaces the next hop attribute of the advertised routes with its own IP address and adds the cluster list attribute to the BGP update message.

The cluster list attribute is used to prevent routing loops in the Route Reflection topology. It contains the list of clusters that the route has traversed, and it is updated by each route reflector that reflects the route.

When a BGP speaker receives a BGP update that includes the cluster list attribute, it checks the list to ensure that it has not already received the route from a route reflector in the same cluster.

So, when a router receives multiple BGP routes from different iBGP peers that have been reflected by a route reflector, it selects the route with the shortest cluster list length. This is because a shorter cluster list indicates that the route has traversed fewer route reflectors and is, therefore, more preferred.

However, it is important to note that the router also considers other BGP attributes, such as the local preference and AS path length, in addition to the cluster list length when selecting the best path. The router selects the BGP route with the highest preference based on all the relevant attributes.

BGP Path selection process

BGP may have multiple paths for the same destination. The best path is the active route that traffic will follow. Here is how the BGP path selection algorithm works:

1. Next hop must be reachable.
2. The route with the highest preference is preferred.
3. The route with the shortest AS Path is preferred.
4. BGP prefers the route with the smallest Origin value.
5. BGP prefers the smallest MED value.

6. Routes learned via EBGP are preferred over routes learned via IBGP.
7. The router selects the route with the smallest IGP metric to the advertised BGP Next Hop.
8. If Route-Reflection is used for IBGP peering, the router selects the route with the shortest Cluster-List length.
9. The router selects the route from the peer with the smallest numerical Router ID.
10. The router selects the route from the peer with the smallest numerical Peer Address.

BGP Synchronization Rule

BGP synchronization rule states that do not use or advertise to an external neighbor a route learned by IBGP until a matching route has been learned from an IGP (OSPF or ISIS).

Route-Maps In-Bound and Out Bound

Inbound Route-map changes the local Router Path selection process. It applies changes to BGP updates received from that specific neighbor. Applying an inbound route-map influences traffic inbound to the BGP router.

Outbound Route-map filter or modify routes being advertised to neighboring routers in a particular direction, usually toward an external network. The outbound route map is configured on the router's interface facing that direction.

The main purpose of an outbound route map is to control the propagation of routing information to external networks. It allows network administrators to manipulate the routing information that is sent to neighboring routers so that only the necessary or desired routes are advertised.

How BGP works?

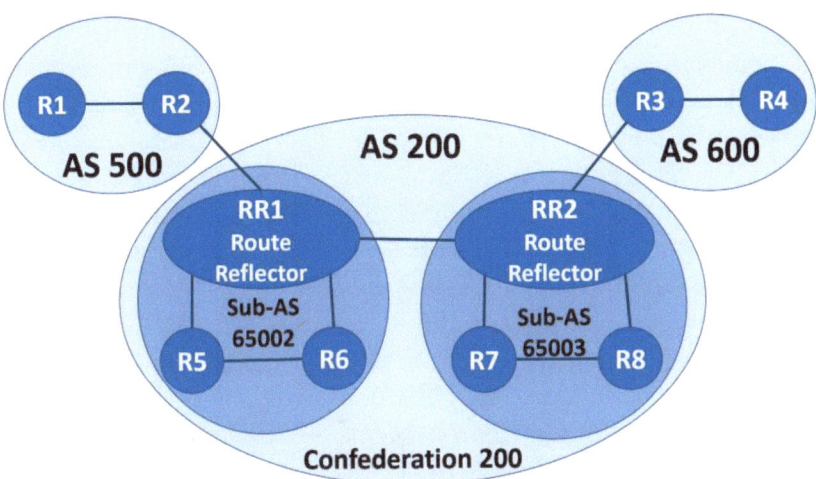

In the summary section, I will tell you some basic concepts of BGP and how these concepts are applied in the real world. BGP is the only protocol in the networking world that connects multiple internet service providers together. In real-life scenarios, you can think of different internet service providers as different and unique autonomous systems. For example, Verizon Business has an AS number of 701, AT&T has AS number of AS7018.

In the above topology diagram, I am using BGP to connect multiple autonomous systems together. Let's start with AS 200. Imagine AS 200 is a large-scale ISP that has hundreds of routers running BGP. In the above picture, I am showing just six routers in AS 200 for the sake of simplicity.

As I have explained earlier in this chapter, BGP routers must be fully meshed to carry complete BGP routing information. To avoid full BGP mesh, and to make the scale manageable, I have divided AS 200 into two sub-autonomous systems, AS 65002 and AS 65003. These sub-autonomous systems have hundreds of routers. This can be further scaled by using route reflectors RR1 and RR2. Here AS 65002 and AS 65003 are private AS numbers. The BGP sessions between RR1 and R5/R6 are IBGP sessions. The BGP session between RR1 and R2 are EBGP sessions. They have significance in AS 200. When external AS 500 or AS 600 peers with AS 200, they see neighboring AS 200. The private AS numbers in AS 200 are not visible to external autonomous systems (AS 500 and AS 600). These fundamental concepts are used by the service providers to establish BGP peering with each other.

BGP interview essentials:

1) Border Gateway Protocol is the only exterior gateway protocol that can exchange routing information among various autonomous systems connected to the internet.
2) BGP is also categorized as a path vector protocol.
3) BGP uses path information, routing policies, and rules to make routing decisions.
4) BGP can also be used within an autonomous system. In such scenarios, it is also called IBGP.
5) BGP is used to exchange and maintain routing information for ISP-level large networks.
6) The current version of BGP is version 4 and it is RFC 4271 which was published in 2006.
7) A BGP can be used in enterprise networks, where these networks are connected to multiple internet service providers or multiple autonomous systems.
8) An enterprise network router that is connected to multiple ISPs (Internet Service Providers) is also called a multihomed router.
9) BGP uses TCP port 179.
10) BGP AS number is a 16-bit number that ranges from 1 to 65535. Range 64512 to 65535 is reserved for private use on the internal networks.
11) AS Numbers can be obtained from Regional Internet Registries (RIR) such as ARIN.
12) There are two types of BGP – EBGB and IBGP.
13) IBGP is run between the BGP routers within an autonomous system.
14) EBGP is run between the BGP routers in different autonomous systems.
15) Administrative distance for IBGP is 200 and the administrative distance for EBGP is 20.
16) BGP uses a three-way handshake process to establish a BGP connection.
17) You cannot run two BGP processes on a single router.
18) BGP neighbors need not be on the same subnet to build the BGP neighbor relationship. BGP uses TCP connections to pass on BGP messages.
19) BGP has different message types – Open, Keepalive, Update, and Notification.

20) Various stages of BGP are Idle, Connect, Active, Open sent, Open confirm, and established.
21) BGP hard reset brings down the neighborship, brings down the TCP connection, and removes all the BGP table entries learned from that neighbor.
22) BGP soft reset does not bring down the BGP neighborship or TCP connections. The local router resends outgoing updates and reprocesses incoming updates adjusting the BGP table based on the current configuration.
23) Local preference is an attribute that decides the path preference to exit the AS to reach a destination. The default value is 100 and a path with higher local preference is preferred.
24) MED is an attribute that influences how other autonomous systems enter our autonomous system. A path with lower MED is preferred.
25) IBGP route learned via IBGP neighbor will not be advertised to another IBGP neighbor. This requires IBGP routers to have a full mesh. To scale this situation, we configure a route reflector server. So, the route reflector server reflects IBGP route information to all IBP route reflector clients.
26) The route reflector can have three types of peering: 1) EBGP neighbor, IBGP client neighbor, and IBGP non-client neighbor.
27) BGP maintains three tables. One is for storing incoming routes from neighbors. One for sending the routes to neighbors. One for installing the routes where you actually find the routes with the next hop address.
28) If BGP is configured on a router that has non-IP interfaces, then BGP cannot get a router id and it assumes 0.0.0.0 router-id.
29) If a BGP neighbor is stuck in an idle state, it could be due to physical connectivity failure, or the neighbor is not defined properly with the respective AS.
30) In connect state, BGP tries to establish a TCP session over port number 179, if it fails to establish the connection, then it goes to an active state, where it tries again to establish a TCP connection.

---

31) Route reflector and confederation techniques are used to share IBGP learned networks with another IBGP neighbor.
32) BGP synchronization helps if your AS provided transit to another AS. In such a scenario BGP should not advertise a route before all routers in your AS learn about the route via IGP. BGP waits until IGP propagates the routes within the AS and then advertises it to external peers. A BGP router with synchronization does not install IBGP-learned routes into its routing table until it validates those routes in IGP.
33) The default BGP Connect Retry timer is 120 seconds.
34) Route dampening affects only EBGP routes.
35) IBGP sessions preserve the next hop attribute.
36) EBGP sessions between confederation sub-autonomous systems do not modify the next hop attribute. Metric and local preferences also stay the same.
37) Roughly 512MB RAM is required for the complete global BGP routing table.
38) The Allow AS feature in BGP allows for routes to be received and processed even if the router detects its own ASN in the AS Path.

6 Multi Protocol Label Switching

MPLS (Multi-Protocol Label Switching)

MPLS technology is one of the new additions to the networking world. I know what you are thinking. I agree it is not so new. Well, this is all relative. MPLS RFC 3031 and RFC 3032 were published in 2001 as compared to BGP RFC 1105 which was published in 1989. MPLS has been around for a while now and is extremely popular among leading internet service providers.

MPLS uses Labels to make forwarding decisions. Each router in the network makes its own forwarding decisions based on the packet's header information. MPLS technology is faster and more efficient as compared to traditional routing. It works on layer 2.5 and it is less CPU intensive.

MPLS typically uses two different types of protocols for label switching:

> LDP – Label Distribution Protocol
> RSVP – Resource Reservation Protocol

LDP (Label Distribution Protocol)

LDP is a protocol that is used for labeling IP packets to facilitate forwarding decisions on an MPLS network. LDP generates and exchanges labels for its IP address prefixes. LDP does not have traffic engineering capabilities and label switched path follows the shortest path using IGP. The label information is exchanged by LDP routers hop by hop. This results in a full mesh where every LDP router has an ingress LSP to every single router on the network.

LDP Neighbors

LDP hello packets are sent as soon as LDP is enabled on a router. These hello messages are sent to a well-known multicast address 224.0.0.2/32 using UDP port 646. There are four types of LDP messages:

Discovery messages are used to announce and maintain the presence of a Label Switch Router (LSR) in a network.
Session messages are used to establish, maintain, and terminate LDP sessions.
Advertising messages are used to create, change, or delete label mappings.
Notification messages are used to relay error information.

LDP Sessions

LDP neighbors exchange label information and transport address via hello messages. Once both neighboring routers learn this information an LDP session is established over a TCP connection. This session is used for advertisement of labels, reachable IP blocks, and interface IP addresses across a link state path.

Forwarding Equivalence Class (FEC)

LDP is used for forwarding traffic using MPLS labels. It uses Forwarding Equivalence Class (FEC) for facilitating data flow through MPLS network and it ensures that each packet is processed consistently across the same physical path. This is no different than the layer three routing. FEC is responsible for forwarding the packet through correct interface and to the appropriate next hop. A router uses loopback address for advertisement as an FEC. The loopback address advertised by LDP is also allocated a label. This helps the router in making forwarding decisions.

LDP Tunneling

In an internet service provider network, there are situations where we have to use traffic engineering and LDP at the same time. Please understand that LDP does not support traffic engineering. It follows the best path based on your interior gateway protocol (ISIS, OSPF). RSVP is a resource reservation protocol that most ISPs use for traffic engineering. LDP traffic can be tunneled through the RSVP network, this is called LDP tunneling.

RSVP (Resource Reservation Protocol)

RSVP is a signaling protocol that supports bandwidth allocation and traffic engineering across MPLS networks. RSVP uses discovery messages to establish neighbor relationships and it uses advertisement messages to maintain LSP path information between all routers. RSVP uses the Constrained Shortest Path First (CSPF) algorithm and Explicit Route Objects (ERO) to calculate routes for traffic traversing on the MPLS network.

RSVP Messages

Let's discuss RSVP messages briefly before explaining the functioning of the protocol in more detail. RSVP has the following messages:

Path
Reserve
PathErr
ResErr
PathTear
ResvTear
ResvConf
Bundle
Ack
Srefresh
Hello
Integrity Challenge
Integrity Response

A picture is worth a thousand words. This topology will help you in understanding the direction and flow of RSVP messages.

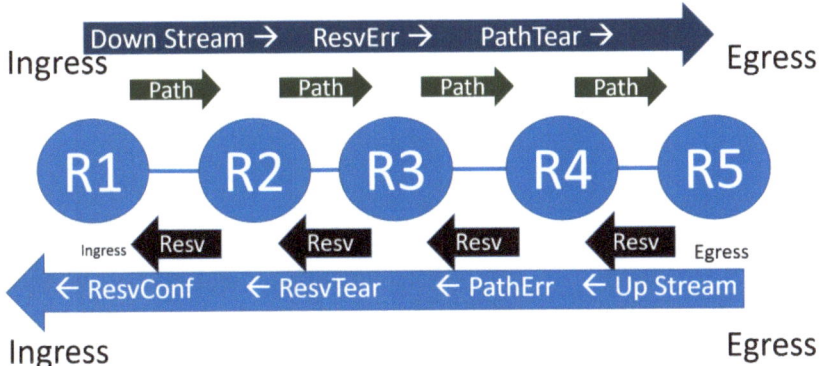

Path Message

As soon as an LSP is configured on an MPLS router, a Path message is generated and forwarded to the downstream egress router. This Path message has the destination IP address of the next hop interface egress router, and it traverses hop by hop.

Resv Message

The Egress router of an LSP generates Resv message towards the upstream ingress router. This message has the destination IP address of the interface of the next upstream router that comes in the path to the ingress router.

PathErr Message

PathErr message is sent to the ingress router from the router encountering an error. These messages are sent upstream hop by hop and the destination IP is the interface IP address of the next upstream router that comes in the path to the ingress router.

ResvErr Message

ResvErr message is sent to the egress router from the router encountering an error. These messages are sent downstream hop by hop and the destination is the interface IP address of the next downstream router interface that comes in the path to the egress router.

PathTear Message

PathTear message is sent to the egress router downstream to tear down an LSP. It traverses hop by hop along the path of the egress router and removes the soft state of an LSP.

ResvTear Message

ResvTear message is sent upstream towards the ingress router. This message is destined to the interface IP address of the next hop in the direction of upstream along the path to the egress router.

ResvConf Message

The ResvConf message is sent from the egress node of the LSP to the ingress node. Once the ingress node receives the ResvConf message, it knows that the LSP has been successfully established and can begin forwarding traffic along the path specified by the LSP.

The purpose of this book is to prepare you for some fundamental concepts. So, I will not deep dive into the nuts and bolts of MPLS networks. To maintain an MPLS network you need to have a deep understanding of routing and how RSVP and LDP work. Now we will discuss some RSVP objects. Now we will discuss some RSVP objects.

Label Object

The Label Object is used to carry a specific label value that will be assigned to the packet by the LSR that receives the signaling message. The label value is used to identify the LSP that the packet belongs to and to determine the path that the packet will take through the network.

Label Request Object

A Label Request Object is a type of object used in the Label Distribution Protocol (LDP) messages exchanged between Label.

Switching Routers (LSRs) to request a label to be assigned to a particular FEC (Forwarding Equivalence Class).

The Label Request Object is used in the Label Mapping message, which is sent by the LSR that has the FEC information to the upstream LSR requesting a label. The Label Request Object is included in this message to request a label to be assigned to the FEC.

When an LSR receives a Label Mapping message with a Label Request Object, it checks if it has a label available that matches the label range requested by the downstream LSR. If a label is available, the LSR assigns the label to the FEC and sends a Label Mapping message with a Label Request Object back to the downstream LSR, along with the assigned label. The downstream LSR then uses this label to forward packets that belong to the FEC.

Explicit Route Object (ERO)

The ERO is included in the RSVP Path message, which is sent by the source node to set up the LSP. The ERO specifies the sequence of LSRs and links that the LSP must traverse, and it can be used to specify a strict or loose path. RSVP messages follow the routes determined by IGP. To determine an LSP a strict or loose ERO can be configured. A strict ERO specifies every single node in between an ingress and egress router. A loose ERO specifies one or multiple LSRs to get to the egress node of an LSP. This may result in multiple transit paths. ERO is part of path messages, and it determines the nodes along the path of an LSP.

Record Route Object

Record route, as the name suggests keeps a record of the nodes which the message has already traversed. RRO can be part of Path or Resv message. The Record Route object (RRO) may be contained in either a Path or a Resv message. RRO is used for loop prevention in an LSP. The record route object is examined by each node, if RRO has an IPv4 address that matches the node's local IP address, a loop is detected, and the message is dropped.

The RRO is included in the RSVP Resv message, which is sent by the downstream LSR to reserve resources along the LSP. The RRO is used to record the path taken by the LSP so that it can be reported back to the sender in the RSVP Path message.

An RRO can contain multiple sub-objects, each specifying a different node along the path. When an LSR receives an RSVP Resv message with an RRO, it adds its own address to the RRO and forwards the message to the next hop along the LSP. This process continues until the message reaches the egress node, which reports the RRO back to the sender in the RSVP Path message.

The RRO is used to verify that the LSP has followed the expected path and to troubleshoot any issues that may arise along the path.

Fast Reroute Object

Fast Reroute (FRR) Object is a type of object used in the Resource Reservation Protocol (RSVP) signaling protocol to provide backup paths for Label Switched Paths (LSPs) in case of link or node failures.

The FRR Object is included in the RSVP Path message and is used to request a detour LSP to be set up as a backup path. The detour LSP is pre-computed and ready to be used in case of a failure in the primary path.

When an LSR receives an RSVP Path message with an FRR Object, it sets up a detour LSP as a backup path for the primary LSP. The detour LSP is pre-computed and ready to be used in case of a failure in the primary path. If a failure occurs, the LSR switches traffic to the detour LSP, which provides uninterrupted service until the primary path is restored.

The FRR Object provides fast recovery from link or node failures, which is critical for applications that require high availability and low latency, such as real-time voice and video. Information within the Fast Reroute object allows each of the routers to consult a local traffic engineering database for calculating a path to the egress router. This information includes a bandwidth reservation, a hop count, LSP priority values, and administrative group knowledge.

Layer 2 MPLS VPN
Internet Service Providers use Layer 2 MPLS VPN to provide Layer 2 or ethernet services to their customers across their MPLS network. This is RFC 2661 and is also known as Martini / L2TP (Layer 2 Tunneling Protocol). This has lower costs, less overhead, and is easy to manage.

Layer 3 MPLS VPN

Internet Service Providers use Layer 3 MPLS VPN to provide Layer 3 services to their customers across their MPLS backbone networks. This is RFC 4364, and it is also called the Kompella protocol. Kompella uses Route Distinguishers and Route Targets to facilitate unique VPN routes for each customer across complex ISP networks.

How does MPLS work?

MPLS enables ISPs to efficiently route traffic by creating specific paths for different types of traffic, such as voice, video, and data. This allows ISPs to optimize network utilization and prioritize traffic based on customer needs. Here, we have an MPLS core network. I will explain how an MPLS network functions in an ISP environment.

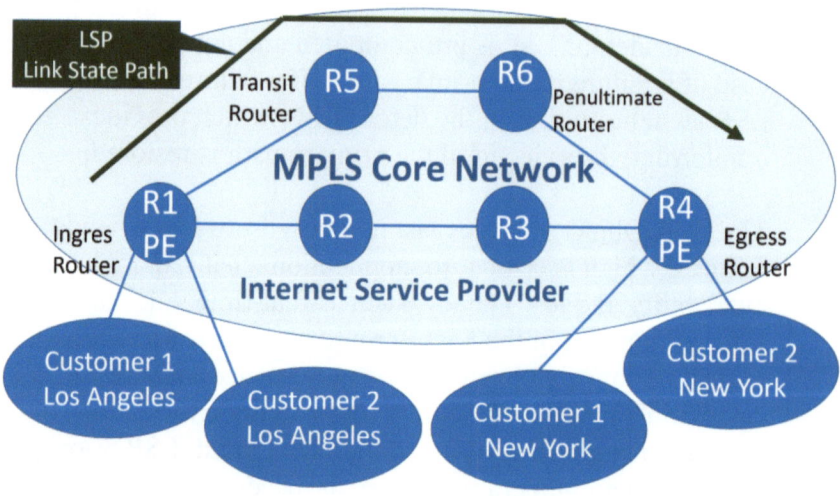

Internet service providers build MPLS core networks to provide value-added services. You may think that the function of an ISP is to provide internet access. This is true to some extent, however, some services like voice, gaming, and live events are time-sensitive. So, it is not just about carrying data packets from point A to point B; it is also important to transport these data packets faster. I will explain this network from an ISP perspective. Routers R1 to R6 are the routers running RSVP. Keep in mind that these routers do run interior gateway protocols such as ISIS, OSPF, and exterior gateway protocol BGP. MPLS is configured over this IP core network to provide value-added services to the customers. In this case, the customer can be a nationwide company that has offices present in multiple states. MPLS network has the capability to push routes of two different customers on the same network. In a traditional network, if customer 1 has a 10.1.1.1 IP address on its network, customer 2 cannot have the same IP address if it is connected to the same core network. However, an MPLS backbone keeps the routes of two customers separate by using a Route Distinguisher. The MPLS RD is used in conjunction with the MPLS VPN technology to provide secure, scalable, and flexible connectivity between geographically dispersed sites. With MPLS VPNs, a service provider can offer virtual private network services to multiple customers using a single network infrastructure while keeping each customer's traffic separate and secure from other customers' traffic.

The Route Distinguisher (RD) is a 64-bit value that is used to identify a unique VPN (Virtual Private Network) route within the service provider network. The RD is used as a prefix to the VPNv4 or VPNv6 prefix to create a unique VPNv4 or VPNv6 route. The RD is assigned to a VPN by the service provider and is used to ensure that VPN routes are unique within the service provider network.

The Route Target (RT), on the other hand, is a BGP extended community attribute that is used to control the distribution of VPN routes across a service provider network. RT is used to associate the VPN routes with a set of VPN customers.

The RT is a 64-bit value that is used to identify a set of VPN customer sites to receive a particular VPN route.

In summary, the Route Distinguisher (RD) is used to ensure that VPN routes are unique within the service provider network, while the Route Target (RT) is used to control the distribution of VPN routes across the service provider network and to associate VPN routes with a set of VPN customers.

Coming back to our discussion on the above network diagram, R1 is an ingress router. This is the router where data enters an LSP. R5 and R6 are transit routers. R4 is an egress router, which is a data exit point for an LSP.

MPLS interview essentials:

1. MPLS is a technology that routers use for forwarding packets based upon labels instead of IP addresses.
2. MPLS supports Ethernet, Frame Relay, X.25.
3. MPLS is layer 2.5 technology. MPLS header resided in between layer 2 and layer 3 of the OSI model, that's where the name layer 2.5 came from.
4. MPLS is very useful for internet service providers because it supports a variety of applications such as Unicast/Multicast routing, virtual private networks, traffic engineering, quality of service, and any transport over MPLS (AToM).
5. MPLS supports forwarding on non-IP protocols because MPLS technologies are applicable to any network layer protocol.
6. MPLS has less overhead compared to conventional routing.
7. MPLS provides BGP free core.
8. MPLS uses TDP or LDP. TDP, Tag Distribution Protocol was developed by Cisco. LDP is a standardized protocol.
9. To run MPLS there are some prerequisites. The interior gateway protocol should be configured and LDP router-id must be reachable. CEF should be in place. CEF is a switching path for MPLS. CEF is pertaining to Cisco routers and its full form is Cisco Express Forwarding. Juniper has a different approach to this. That discussion, I will leave for a different book.
10. P router is a provider router, and it does not have customer network routes.
11. PE router is a Provider Edge router, and it carries customer network routes. MP-iBGP is required on the PE router.
12. MPLS performs three basic functions on a label – PUSH -Adding a label, POP – Removing the label, and SWAP – Changing the label.
13. You can convert your PE router to P by removing the BGP configuration. Once the BGP configuration is removed there will not be any exchange of routing information.

14. Penultimate hop popping is a method of reducing label lookups on egress router. It is performed by one hop before the egress router.
15. TTL propagation is a method of copying the TTL value from the IP header to the MPLS header.
16. Per platform label space indicates the labels assigned to packets based on the destination network.
17. Per Interface Label space indicates the labels assigned based on the destination network and the router interface.
18. The Implicit Null label (Label 3) is used to instruct the last but one (penultimate) router in the Label Switched Path (LSP) to remove the label from the packet before forwarding it to the final destination. This is known as Penultimate Hop Popping (PHP).
19. Explicit Null (Label 0) is used for QOS marking and it disables PHP behavior.
20. The "Aggregate Null" label is a label value (usually represented by a specific label value, often 3 or 0) used to indicate that no label-based action should be taken. When a router encounters an "Aggregate Null" label at the top of the label stack, it doesn't perform any label-based forwarding action. Instead, it typically pops (removes) the "Aggregate Null" label and forwards the packet based on the IP header.

LDP interview essentials:

1. LDP generates and exchanges labels with neighboring routers. Labels are generated for the prefixes and are advertised to neighbors.
2. LDP establishes link state paths (LSPs) through a network by using interior gateway routing (IGP) information.
3. LDP uses the multicast address 224.0.0.2.
4. LDP uses UDP port 646 for creating neighbor. relationships. It uses a TCP port for exchanging label information.
5. LDP router has a unique LSR ID (Label Switch Router).
6. LDP selects the highest loopback interface address as LSR ID. If there is no loopback address configured, the highest IP address on a physical interface is selected for LSR ID. If there is no loopback address configured, the highest IP address on the physical interface is the next best choice for LSR ID.
7. LDP hello interval is 5 seconds, and the hold timer is 15 seconds.
8. If two LDP neighbors have different hold times configured, the smaller hold value is used.
9. LDP uses messages to establish and remove label mappings and to report errors. LDP messages use a Type, Length, and Value (TLV) encoding scheme. There are four types of LDP messages – Discovery Messages, Session Messages, Advertisements Messages, and Notification Messages.
10. Discovery messages are hello messages which announce and maintain the presence of an LDP router on the network.
11. LDP uses two different discovery procedures, - Basic Discovery and Extended Discovery. A basic discovery message is a hello message sent to a directly connected LDP router as UDP packets on port 646. Extended discovery messages are LDP-targeted hello messages destined for a specific LDP router that is not directly connected.

12. Session messages establish, maintain, and terminate sessions between LDP peers. An LDP router uses an LDP initialization procedure through hello messages. When the initialization procedure is complete, the two LDP routers establish a neighbor relationship and are ready to exchange advertisement messages.

13. LDP advertisement messages create, delete and change label mappings for forwarding equivalence classes (FEC). The router requests a label mapping from a neighboring router, and it advertises a label mapping to a router, in case it wants a neighbor to use a label.

14. LDP sends notification messages to report errors and other events. There are two types of LDP notification messages: Error notifications and Advisory notifications.

15. LDP is only responsible for the topmost label which is the IGP label. MP-iBGP is responsible for the vpnv4 label.

16. LDP graceful restart enables a router whose LDP control plane is undergoing a restart to continue to forward traffic while recovering its state from neighboring routers. It also enables a router on which helper mode is enabled to assist a neighboring router that is attempting to restart LDP.

17. LDP loop detection can be implemented in two modes – Maximum hop count and Path vector. To implement loop detection in an MPLS network, one has to enable loop detection on every LSR in the MPLS domain.

18. The LDP IGP synchronization feature ensures that the LDP protocol is fully converged before the IGP path is used for LSPs'. This feature is available for directly connected LDP neighbors. If LDP is down and IGP is up, the router will not forward the packets on that link.

19. LDP uses Message Digest 5 (MD5) authentication.

20. To reduce the number of label bindings on an LSR, you can either control the advertisements of label bindings via LDP in the outbound direction, or you can filter the incoming label bindings.

21. If two routers running LDP have two or more equal-cost routes, there will be only one LDP session.

RSVP interview essentials:

1. RSVP is an IETF (Internet Engineering Task Force) standard that was first introduced in 1991.
2. Resource Reservation Protocol is a protocol that establishes Label Switched Paths (LSPs) with specific QoS parameters. RSVP is flexible and provides more precise control over network resources as compared to LDP.
3. RSVP was designed to address the problem of providing guaranteed quality of service (QoS) in IP networks.
4. RSVP allows devices to request and reserve network resources, such as bandwidth or QoS, in advance.
5. RSVP is a signaling protocol that uses messages to reserve network resources and establish paths for data flows.
6. RSVP can be used in conjunction with other protocols, such as MPLS (Multiprotocol Label Switching) and DiffServ (Differentiated Services), to provide better QoS and traffic engineering capabilities.
7. RSVP can be used to reserve resources for a variety of applications, including multimedia streaming, voice-over-IP (VoIP), and real-time video conferencing.
8. The most recent version of RSVP, RSVP-TE (RSVP Traffic Engineering), was introduced in 2001 and includes additional features for more precise traffic engineering and resource allocation.
9. RSVP is not widely used in enterprise networks due to its complexity and the lack of support for it in many networking devices.

7 Multicast

Multicast

Multicast is a group communication that is addressed to a group of hosts.

When a multicast source is not known, it is represented by 0.0.0.0 or "*". So this representation is also called (*,G).

Multicast addresses and address ranges:

The Internet Assigned Numbers Authority (IANA) has reserved a range of address space specifically for multicast communications. This range is from 224.0.0.0 to 239.255.255.255.

224.0.0.1/32 represents all IP hosts on the subnet. (Each router and PC).

224.0.0.2/32 represents all IP routers on the network. Hosts (Computers, servers, laptops) do not process these messages.

224.0.0.5/32 is an address reserved for OSPF routers.

224.0.0.6/32 is an address reserved for OSPF designated and backup designated routers (DR's and BDR's).

224.0.0.9/32 is reserved for RIP version 2.

224.0.0.13/32 is reserved for PIM version 2.

224.0.0.18/32 is reserved for VRRP, Virtual Router Redundancy Protocol.

224.0.0.22/32 is reserved for IGMP version 3.

232.0.0.0/8 is reserved for SSM, Source Specific Multicasting.

233.0.0.0/8 is reserved for GLOP. This address range facilitates the capability to map an autonomous system with multicast addresses.

239.0.0.0/8 is reserved for LAN. This is like private IPv4 addresses.

Reverse Path Forwarding

Reverse Path Forwarding is a mechanism to avoid forwarding loops in a multicast environment. As we know, routing is destination based. In a multicast environment, data is sent from one source to a group of receivers. This can result in forwarding loops. The default behavior of a router running multicast is that it forwards data to all interfaces except the one from which it receives it. RPF is a mechanism that checks the route to the source and makes sure that the interface that received the request from the source is the best path in the reverse direction. Hence this justifies the name RPF.

IGMP

IGMP is an abbreviation for Internet Group Management Protocol. This is a protocol that facilitates communication between a receiver and a multicast router. A receiver sends a request to the multicast router to join a multicast group. The IGMP protocol uses the following IGMP messages:

Membership reports are sent by a device to a multicast router. A device sends this request message to a multicast router to become a member of a multicast group.

"Leave group" messages are used to leave a multicast group. These messages are sent from a device to a multicast router.

General membership queries are sent by a multicast router to all the devices on the network to update multicast group membership for all groups on the network.

Group-specific membership queries are sent to a specific multicast group.

PIM

PIM stands for Protocol Independent Multicast. Multicast communications can be one to many or many to many. PIM is protocol independent because it does not have any native algorithms to discover network topology. It uses the routing information generated by other routing protocols. PIM has two main modes of configuration, PIM Dense Mode and PIM Sparse Mode.

PIM Dense Mode

Multicast dense mode is efficient in case there is significant number of receivers. It initiates multicast traffic under the assumption that each receiver on the multicast network requires data traffic coming from source. So initially all the links are flooded with multicast traffic. There are certain segments of the network which do not have any receivers and they do not need multicast traffic. So, the routers which do not need this multicast data traffic will send a prune request to the source. On the contrary there are network segments which have receivers, the routers connected to these segments will reply to the source with IGMP join request.

PIM Sparse Mode

PIM sparse mode is used in case the number of receivers is less. There is an RP (Rendezvous Point) router that acts as a communication point between source and receivers. RP router keeps information about sources of multicast groups and receivers' requests. In simple words source and receiver forward multicast data traffic via RP router.
RP router can be configured in the following options:
Static RP
Auto RP
Bootstrap RP

Multicast Forwarding

During this discussion, we will delve into the process by which a multicast network forwards data packets from the source to the intended receivers. To prevent loops in the network, multicast networks utilize a technique known as reverse path forwarding (RPF).

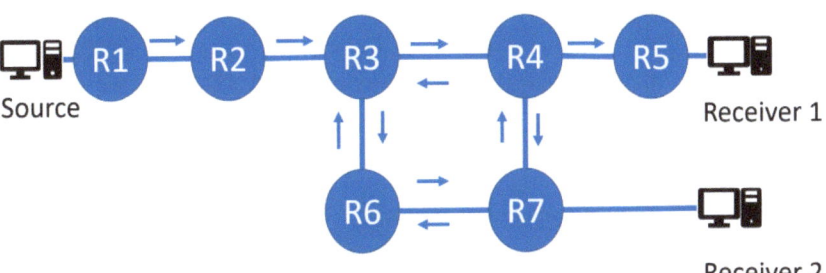

Now let's discuss the communication from source to receiver 1 and receiver 2.

The multicast source is connected to R1. The source will send multicast traffic to Receiver 1 and Receiver 2.

R1 will transmit the data stream to R2 and R2 will transmit the multicast data stream to R3 using the multicast forwarding procedure.

R3 has two multicast neighbors R4 and R6. So, R3 sends a similar stream to R4 and R6.

R4 and R6 received the same multicast stream.

R4 checks for neighbors on downstream interfaces and finds routers R5 and R7. So, R4 sends the multicast data stream to R5 and R7. Remember, that R4 is receiving this stream from R3, so it will not send that same information back to R3.

R6 router is connected to only one downstream router R7, so it will send that multicast stream to R7.

If you observe carefully, R7 receive the same stream from R4 and R6.

R7 will receive the stream from R6 and will forward it to R4.

R7 will receive the stream from R4 and will forward it to R6.

This scenario has created a loop between R3, R4, R6, and R7. This loop can be resolved by the reverse path forwarding method.

As we know, router R7 receives the same data packed from R6 and R4. R7 knows that it is receiving data packets on its two different interfaces from the same source IP address. R7 will use RPF to find the best path to the source IP address. Once it determines the best path to the source of the data packet, it forwards that data packet to all downstream interfaces. On the contrary, if the RPF check determines that the path to the source IP address is not the best path, it will not forward these multicast data packets and these packets will be dropped. So, in the case of R7, there are two routes to the source:

R7→R4→R3→R2→R1→Source

R7→R6→R3→R2→R1→Source (Best Path to Source)

R7 receives the same data packet from R4 and R6.
R7 needs to decide which one to keep. The one from R4 or the one from R6.

In this case the RPF routing table determines that the best path from R7 to source is via R6. So R7 will keep the data packet received from R6 and forward it to the downstream router R4. R7 will drop the data packet it has received from R4, because in RPF routing this is not the best route to the source.

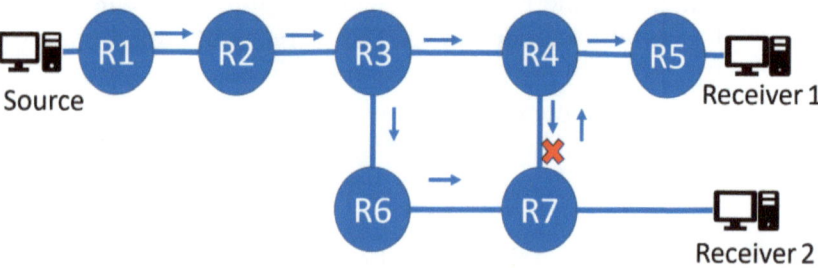

Dense-Mode Forwarding

Dense mode multicast routing protocol is used in an environment with a large number of receivers. Here is a dense-mode multicast network.

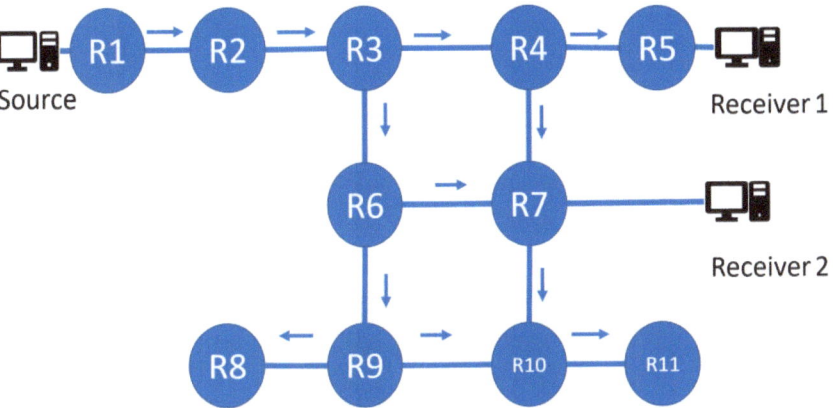

The source connected to R1 sends multicast data packets to receivers connected to routers R5 and R7. All the routers on the network are configured for multicast dense mode. So, all the network segments are flooded with multicast traffic. As you can see, there are routers that are not connected to any receiver, but they are still receiving multicast data packets. Such routers send prune messages to upstream routers and prune themselves from the multicast forwarding path. The flood and prune process happens every three minutes in Juniper routers. This ensures that if a new receiver is added to the network, it receives traffic from the source.

Sparse Mode Forwarding

Sparse mode forwarding is used if we have a large number of sources in the network.

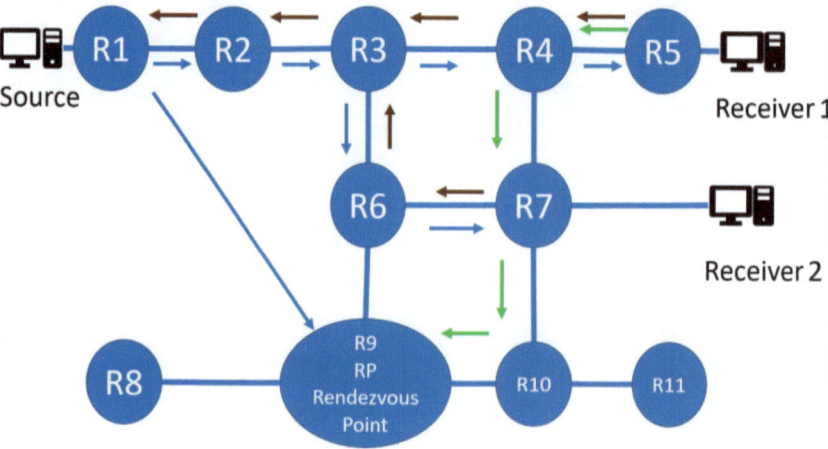

A multicast router in a sparse mode, requests for the data stream from the source. In sparse mode there is a rendezvous point also known as an RP router, that acts like a connection point between the sources and receivers in multicast networks. In the above example, R9 is the RP router. Receivers connected to R5 and R7 sent a request to connect to the multicast group address. These requests are sent to the RP router. R9 router, also known as the RP router, receives multicast.

traffic from router R1 (Connected to the source). RP router facilitates the connection between the source and receivers on the network. Once RP receives multicast data traffic from the source and the "requests to connect to multicast group address" from receivers, the multicast traffic starts forwarded through this network. If for receivers the best route to source is not via the RP router, then R5 and R7 prune themselves from the shared tree by sending a prune message to RP router.

Multicast interview essentials:

1) Multicast is used to send data from one source to multiple receivers.
2) IGMP stands for Internet Group Management Protocol, and it facilitates communication between the host and multicast routers.
3) PIM is a multicast routing protocol that is used to build multicast distribution trees in a network. It supports both dense mode and sparse mode multicast routing and can be used with both IPv4 and IPv6 networks. PIM enables routers to discover and join multicast groups, and to propagate multicast traffic to other routers in the network based on the multicast distribution tree.
4) MLD (Multicast Listener Discovery) is a protocol used by IPv6 hosts to inform their neighboring routers of their multicast group membership. When a host wants to join a multicast group, it sends an MLD message to its local router, which then forwards the message to other routers in the network. MLD enables routers to build multicast distribution trees and to forward multicast traffic only to those parts of the network where there are interested receivers.
5) IGMP Snooping and CGMP provide communication between the router and switch.
6) In IGMP version 1, messages used are Membership queries and membership reports.
7) In IGMP version 2, messages used are query, report, and leave.
8) Multicast distribution tree specifies the path between the source and receiver to forward multicast traffic.
9) There are two types of multicast distribution trees, Source tree, and shared tree.
10) Source tree is used in both PIM Sparse Mode and Dense Mode.
11) Source tree uses the source as the root of the multicast tree and receivers act as branches. It is also called the shortest path tree because it uses the shortest path

between the source and receiver. Every router in the source tree will add (S, G) entries.

12) In (S, G) S is a source or sender IP address and G is a group or multicast address 224.5.5.5.

13) Shared tree is used in PIM sparse mode only. It uses the Rendezvous point as the root of multicast and the shortest path tree is created between Source & RP and Receiver & RP. Every router in the source tree will add (*, G). Here * denotes all sources and G is multicast IP address 224.5.5.5.

14) PIM is a protocol used between the routers to forward multicast traffic. PIM can be implemented in PIM dense mode and PIM sparse mode.

15) The Link-local multicast range is reserved with 224.0.0.0/24. They have a TTL of 1and they cannot be forwarded outside of the link. Such multicast IP addresses are used in protocols. For example, OSPF uses 224.0.0.5.

16) Source-Specific Multicast address range is reserved with 232.0.0.0/8. These addresses are used for discovering the unicast address of the server that is generating multicast traffic.

17) GLOP Multicast Address range is reserved with 233.0.0.0/8. Interestingly there is no abbreviation for GLOP. GLOP multicast addresses are used by companies that have their own public AS numbers.
For example, AS number =21544
Convert AS number decimal to Hexadecimal.
21544 is converted to 5428.
Convert the first two digits and last two digits of hexadecimal to decimal.
So, 54 is converted to 84, and 28 is converted to 40.
The multicast address is 233.84.40.0/24.

18) The Private Multicast Address range is reserved with 239.0.0.0/8. This multicast range is like private IPv4 addresses. These are also known as administratively scoped addresses.

19) IGMP version 3 supports SSM (Source Specific Multicasting).

8 Securing Networks

Security is a very critical aspect of a network. Network devices such as routers and switches are responsible for facilitating internet to LAN users. So, any router that is connected to the internet is open to internet traffic and anyone who has access to the internet can get to these devices. It is imperative to secure routing and switching devices from internal and external users.

Routers have in-built security. They can permit or deny traffic flows based on the following four components:

Source IP Address
Source Port
Destination IP Address
Destination Port.

Cisco routers use IP access lists. Juniper routers use an in-built firewall feature to secure the network from security threats.

Firewalls

A firewall is a network security system that monitors and controls incoming and outgoing network traffic based on predetermined security rules. The main purpose of a firewall is to block unauthorized access to a computer or network while still allowing authorized traffic to pass through.

Here's how a firewall typically works:

The firewall sits between a private internal network and the public Internet, acting as a gatekeeper between the two.

All traffic passing through the firewall is analyzed and compared to a set of predefined rules.

If the traffic meets the criteria of a rule, it is allowed to pass through the firewall and reach its intended destination.

If the traffic does not meet the criteria of a rule, it is either blocked or redirected to a different destination.

The firewall can also be configured to monitor traffic in real-time and alert network administrators of any suspicious activity, such as attempts to access restricted resources or unusual traffic patterns.

There are several types of firewalls, including network firewalls, host-based firewalls, and application firewalls. Network firewalls are the most common type and are typically implemented as hardware devices or software applications that run on a dedicated server. Host-based firewalls, on the other hand, run on individual computers and protect them from local network traffic. Application firewalls are designed to protect specific applications, such as web browsers or email clients, from attacks.

Overall, firewalls are an essential component of network security, providing an extra layer of protection against unauthorized access, malware, and other cyber threats.

DMZ

DMZ stands for Demilitarized Zone, which is a network segment that is isolated from the rest of the network and exposed to the public internet. It is a security feature commonly used to add an additional layer of protection to a company's network infrastructure.

The DMZ is typically located between the internal network and the internet, and it is used to host servers that need to be accessed from outside the organization, such as web servers, email servers, or FTP servers. By isolating these servers in the DMZ, it helps to reduce the risk of attacks against the internal network.

In a typical DMZ configuration, there are two firewalls. The first firewall separates the DMZ from the internet, and the second firewall separates the DMZ from the internal network. Traffic is allowed to flow from the DMZ to the internal network, but traffic from the internal network to the DMZ is restricted, and traffic from the internet to the internal network is blocked.

The servers in the DMZ are usually configured with limited access rights, and they are only permitted to communicate with specific servers or services in the internal network. This helps to prevent unauthorized access and to limit the potential damage if one of the servers in the DMZ is compromised.

Overall, the DMZ is an important security feature that provides an additional layer of protection for critical servers that need to be accessible from the internet. By isolating these servers in a separate network segment, it helps to reduce the risk of attacks and to protect the internal network from unauthorized access.

Cyber security is another field, and it is a topic for another book. However, as a network engineer you should be familiar with some basic security concepts and terminologies which you are going to use with your network security peers.

DOS Attacks

Denial of Service (DoS) is a type of cyber-attack that aims to make a website or online service unavailable to its intended users. The attack is typically carried out by flooding the targeted system with a high volume of traffic or requests, overwhelming its capacity to handle them and causing the system to crash or become unavailable.

DoS attacks can take various forms, including:

Network flood attacks: These attacks flood the network connection of the target with traffic, such as UDP or ICMP packets, rendering it unable to handle legitimate traffic.

Application attacks: These attacks exploit vulnerabilities in the application layer of a system, such as a web server or database, to make it unavailable to users.

Protocol attacks: These attacks exploit weaknesses in network protocols, such as TCP or DNS, to make a network or system unavailable.

Distributed Denial of Service (DDoS) attacks

These attacks involve a coordinated effort from multiple sources, often using a botnet, to flood a target system with traffic from multiple directions.

DoS attacks can have serious consequences for the targeted system and its users. For example, they can disrupt critical services, cause financial losses, and damage the reputation of the affected organization. To protect against DoS attacks, organizations can implement a range of measures, such as firewalls, intrusion detection and prevention systems, and traffic filtering. It is also important to have a response plan in place in case of an attack.

Ransomware

Ransomware is a type of malicious software that encrypts a victim's files, making them inaccessible and demands payment in exchange for the decryption key needed to restore the files. The payment is usually demanded in a cryptocurrency, such as Bitcoin, to make it difficult to trace.

Malware

Malware is a type of malicious software that is designed to harm a computer system or network, steal sensitive data, or gain unauthorized access to a system. Malware can take various forms, including viruses, worms, Trojan horses, ransomware, and spyware.

Here are some of the common types of malware:

Viruses

These are programs that can replicate themselves and spread from one computer to another, often by infecting executable files.

Worms

These are standalone programs that can replicate themselves and spread through networks, often by exploiting vulnerabilities in software or operating systems.

Trojan horses

These are programs that appear to be legitimate but contain hidden malicious code that can damage or steal data from a system.

Spyware

This is software that is designed to gather information about a user's online activities without their knowledge or consent.

Malware can have serious consequences for the victim, including data loss, financial losses, and damage to reputation. To protect against malware, it is important to have up-to-date antivirus software, avoid opening suspicious emails or attachments, use strong passwords, and keep software and operating systems up to date with the latest security patches.

If malware is suspected or detected on a system, it is important to isolate the affected system from the network and seek professional assistance to remove the malware and recover any lost data.

How does network security work?

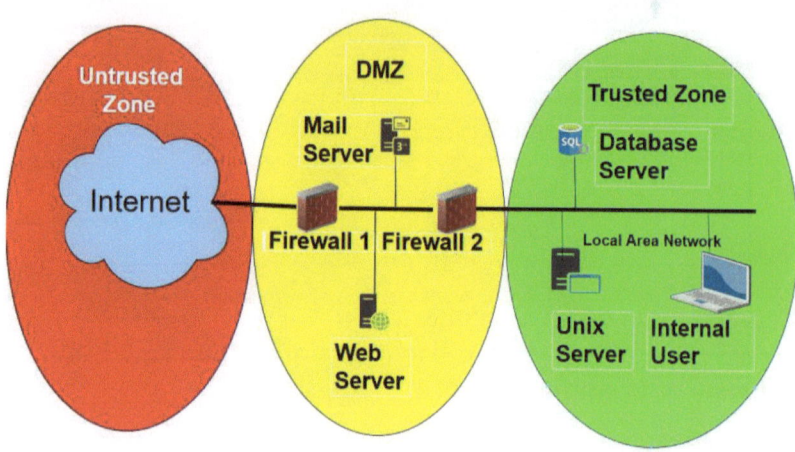

In the above topology, we are using two firewalls. Firewall 1 is facing the internet and Firewall 2 is facing local area network. Firewall 2 protects local area network. Firewall 1 controls the traffic flows between the internet and demilitarized zone. This is a very common security topology to secure enterprise environment. The yellow highlighted area, between Firewall 1 and Firewall 2 is called Demilitarized Zone. This is the zone where you keep your web server. The red highlighted area is called Untrusted Zone. The green highlighted area is called Trusted Zone. This is your LAN, and this zone is supposed to be the most secure. Your database servers, active directory servers and other application servers reside in trusted zone. Most security engineers work with firewall policies to control network traffic coming from untrusted zone to trusted zone and vice versa.

Security Interview Essentials

1. A firewall is a security device or software that monitors and controls incoming and outgoing network traffic. It can be used to enhance router security by blocking unauthorized access attempts, filtering malicious traffic, and enforcing security policies.

2. Authentication is the process of verifying the identity of a user or device, while authorization is the process of determining what resources or actions that user or device is allowed to access or perform.

3. 2FA is a security method that requires users to provide two forms of identification to access a system or device, such as a username/password and a security token or biometric factor.

4. MAC filtering is a technique used to restrict access to a network based on the MAC addresses of devices. It can be used to enhance router security by only allowing trusted devices with known MAC addresses to connect to the network, reducing the risk of unauthorized access.

5. SNMP (Simple Network Management Protocol) is a protocol used to monitor and manage network devices, including routers. It is important to secure it because it can be used by attackers to gather sensitive information, such as device configurations and network topology.

6. A honeypot is a decoy system or service designed to lure attackers and gather information about their techniques and tools. It can be used to enhance router security by diverting attackers away from the actual network and providing insight into their tactics and motivations.

7. A vulnerability scanner is a tool used to identify potential security weaknesses or vulnerabilities on a network. It can be used to enhance router security by regularly scanning the network for known vulnerabilities and providing recommendations for remediation.

8. SSL (Secure Socket Layer) and TLS (Transport Layer Security) are both cryptographic protocols used to secure network connections, but TLS is the successor to SSL and is more secure. TLS supports stronger encryption algorithms and has better protection against attacks.

9. A Man in The Middle attack is an attack in which an attacker intercepts communication between two parties and can eavesdrop on, modify, or inject data into the communication. It can be prevented or detected by using encryption and authentication methods, using trusted certificates, and implementing network monitoring tools.

10. A default gateway is the network device that connects a local network to the internet or another network. It is important to secure it because it controls access to the outside network and can be a target for attackers trying to gain unauthorized access.

11. Network segmentation is the process of dividing a network into smaller segments or subnetworks to improve performance, security, and management. It can be used to enhance router security by separating sensitive systems or services from less critical ones, reducing the risk of a security breach spreading across the network.

12. Cisco routers use ACLs to filter traffic based on various criteria, such as IP address, port number, protocol type, and interface. ACLs can be applied to inbound or outbound traffic on a router interface, or on a specific network protocol.

13. In Cisco routers there are two types of ACLs: standard and extended. Standard ACLs only filter traffic based on source IP address, while extended ACLs can filter traffic based on source and destination IP address, as well as other criteria such as protocol type and port number.

14. Juniper ACLs are created using the firewall filter feature. Firewall filters can be applied to various types of traffic, such as interface traffic, routing protocols, and VPN traffic. Firewall filters consist of one or more terms that define the criteria for matching traffic and the actions to take on the matching traffic. Each term has a unique name, a match condition, and an action. The match conditions can be based on various criteria, such as source and destination IP addresses, ports, protocols, and VLAN tags. The action can be to accept, reject, discard, or forward the traffic.